Sinn Féin

A Century of Struggle

Céad Bliain ar son na saoirse

Published 2005 by Sinn Féin,

44 Parnell Square, Dublin 1, Ireland.

Tel: +353 1 8726100; Fax: +353 1 8783595

Email: sales@sinnfeinbookshop.com / sfadmin@eircom.net

Website: www.sinnfeinbookshop.com / www.sinnfein.ie

Softback ISBN: 0-9542946-1-0

Hardback ISBN: 0-9542946-2-9

Introduction by Uachtarán Sinn Féin Gerry Adams

This book is a key element of Céad Bliain Sinn Féin, our party's celebration of its hundredth anniversary. I want to thank and commend all those who were involved in putting this book together — Micheál MacDonncha, Mark Joyce, Aengus Ó Snodaigh, Shane Mac Thomáis, Dawn Doyle, Brian Dowling, Matt Treacy, Mark Dawson, John Hedges and Eric Eckhart.

This anniversary is about education and debate. It is about the re-popularising of republicanism. It is about learning the lessons of a century of struggle. It's also about taking pride in what we are about. And what we have achieved. But most important of all this year is about Sinn Féin taking more decisive steps forward toward our goal of a united, free and independent Ireland.

In this centenary year we remember especially all those republicans who lived, worked and died for freedom. We remember them - we remember them all with great pride and love.

Tá na daoine seo ó achan cearn den oileán - an tuaisceart agus an deisceart - an oirthear agus an iarthar - cathrach agus tuathanach - sean agus óg - fir agus mná.

Their absence reminds us of how much we have lost in the course of this struggle. Each one was a unique, irreplaceable human being. These were ordinary men and women who in extraordinary and difficult circumstances found the inner strength, determination and courage to stand against injustice and oppression, to demand the rights and entitlements of the Irish people.

Our task - our duty - is to make their vision their dream - a reality.

That means defining and redefining our republicanism for today's world - for today's Ireland. Those who established Sinn Féin 100 years ago; those who fought on the streets of Dublin in 1916 and later against the might of the British Empire; and those who raised the flag of resistance in each subsequent generation, did so in circumstances that differed and changed as the years rolled past.

This is not 1905. It is 2005. It is the 21st century.

Republicanism today, and our dream, our vision, our aisling of the future reflects our contemporary experience; the inspiration provided by the heroes of this phase of struggle - Máire Drumm and Bobby Sands, Eddie Fullerton and Sheena Campbell and John Davey and many others; and by our political objectives for this time.

Sinn Féin is an Irish Republican party. Our strategy to achieve a united, independent Ireland marks us out from other Irish political parties. In 2005 we launched a campaign for the Irish government to bring forward a Green Paper on Irish Unity. Our primary political objectives are an end to partition, an end to the union, the construction of a new national democracy - a new republic - on the island of Ireland, and reconciliation between Orange and Green. But we are not prepared to wait until we have achieved these goals for people to have their rights to a decent home, to a job and a decent wage, to decent public services like health and education, and a safer cleaner environment.

We are carrying the honoured name of Sinn Féin into the 21st century. And after a century of struggle, we are preparing for success. When will we get our United Ireland? When will Ireland have independence? There's only one answer to that. We will get it when our combined efforts, our combined strength, our determination make its achievement unstoppable. We will not settle for less. And the greater our efforts - the more quickly we will achieve our goals.

Let us move the struggle forward. Let us continue, despite the difficulties - to reach out to Unionism to build a just and lasting peace on our island. Let us continue with our efforts to make the peace process work.

We are prepared to join with those in other parties and none, who share our vision of a new Ireland. We ask them to walk with us; to work with us; to move forward with us toward the Republican and democratic goals of unity and freedom and equality.

I have mentioned the dream that motivates us. Anyone who wants to win a struggle has to have a dream. The dream that things can be different. That they can be better. But we are not only dreamers. We are doers. We know we can make the difference.

In this Céad Bliain we are determined to fulfil the promise of the Proclamation, and the objective for which Sinn Féin was founded - a free, independent, sovereign Ireland.

Ar aghaidh linn le chéile.

Adhmáil

Ba mhaith liom buíochas a ghabháil le gach duine a chabhraigh liom san obair seo, ach go háirithe le Aengus Ó Snodaigh, Shane Mac Thomáis, Dawn Doyle, Brian Dowling, Matt Treacy, Mark Dawson, Eric Eckhart, John Hedges. Buíochas leis an bhfoireann in *An Phoblacht* agus le foireann Sinn Féin i dTeach Laighean. Is le Mark Joyce, a rinne an leagan amach, an leabhar seo chomh maith. Ach is liomsa cibé botún atá ann.

Mícheál MacDonncha

Editor's Introduction

This book is an attempt to provide an overview of one hundred years of Sinn Féin. A definitive history of Sinn Féin has yet to be written and this is not such a book. Instead, this book attempts to document a century of struggle through the contemporary words of Republicans themselves. The emphasis is on ideas, policies and strategies, on the development of a struggle and the thinking that lay behind it.

For much of the period covered, Sinn Féin's role was very much dominated by its political support for the armed struggle of the Irish Republican Army (IRA). That is not because of any innate war-like or 'terrorist' quality in Irish Republicans. It was a direct result of the violence of the terrorist British government in Ireland. Therefore, armed struggle naturally figures prominently in this book. However, this is not a history of the IRA or of the overall armed conflict since 1969.

No doubt omissions will be pointed out by people coming from many different political perspectives — including Republicans. It has been a very difficult task to encompass a century of struggle in a single volume such as this. The range of Sinn Féin activity in any one period can only be touched upon. This is particularly true of the later years as Sinn Féin expanded to a truly All-Ireland party, campaigning on a wide range of social and economic issues. While the final years covered in this work are dominated by developments in the peace process, this was also a time when Sinn Féin extended its activities greatly. Space did not allow that range of political work to be fully reflected.

This book does not purport to be an academic work. It was compiled by a Sinn Féin activist in intervals during ongoing full-time political work. It was not possible to compile a comprehensive list of sources, although sources for most of the text are given in the introductory paragraphs.

In compiling this book I was struck once again by the importance of a newspaper to any revolutionary party. Sinn Féin was censored by both partitionist states in Ireland during much of the century covered here. It is still subject to media self-censorship and misrepresentation. Therefore, Republican newspapers from throughout the last 100 years are an invaluable source, and often the only source, for Sinn Féin ideas and actions. Since 1970, Irish Republicans have maintained unbroken the publication of their newspapers — *An Phoblacht* in Dublin and *Republican News* in Belfast from 1970, and the amalgamated paper since 1979. I was privileged to be editor of the paper between 1990 and 1996 and I would like to pay tribute to all who have worked for the paper in any capacity. In a very real sense, they made history, as these pages testify.

The political project of Sinn Féin which began on 28 November 1905 is still very much a work in progress. And the celebration of Céad Bliain Sinn Féin is part of that work, another element in the ongoing struggle for Irish unity and independence. This book chronicles the fight against Partition, for Irish unity and for an end to British rule in our country. It reflects the struggle for a new Ireland based on social and economic justice, an Ireland of equals.

This book is dedicated to all those who have participated in the struggle for freedom — those who died, those who suffered imprisonment, those who lived and worked to achieve the Republic. It is especially dedicated to those unsung heroes who have done the mundane, routine political work that is essential for the life of any party. Often members of Sinn Féin have done that ordinary work in extraordinary circumstances. But they have been sustained by an ideal and by a sense of comradeship that has endured through the darkest of days.

Tá súil agam go mbainfidh gach duine a léann an leabhar seo taitneamh as. Tá súil agam freisin go spreagann sé daoine chun páirt a ghlacadh san obair ar son na saoirse.

Mícheál MacDonncha and Mark Dawson in the production office of An Phoblacht / Republican News.

Members of the Dungannon Club, 1906

The Early Years
1905-1909

Arthur Griffith

them to forget their principles, whether from weakness or corruption, and afforded the anti-national party a means to triumph over the apparent ineffectiveness of Ireland's aspirations. It was then that, in the general confusion of ruinous lies and credulity, it was found necessary to establish some platform upon which Nationalists might meet who recognised the folly and treason to Ireland of voluntarily recognising a king who was ruling in defiance of our Constitution.

Owing to the work of the National Council, King Edward was refused an address from Dublin Corporation. This was the first time since the invasion of Ireland by Henry II in the 12th century that an official Dublin body performed such a patriotic act. Its influence and its success in Dublin strengthened the hand of every Nationalist in the country. Emboldened by such success the members of the National Council thought it a pity that such a body should be dissolved at the conclusion of the royal visit...

Then there appeared in Ireland a pamphlet of extraordinary political ability, which at once flew over the country and established for its author a reputation for statesmanship such as no Irishman has since Parnell. 'The Resurrection of Hungary' has set Ireland thinking of the policy of Sinn Féin. It is this policy that our convention has chiefly to consider at this conference.

Arthur Griffith, author of 'The Resurrection of Hungary' (1904), then presented a detailed programme which was later published as 'The Sinn Féin Policy'.

No law and no series of laws can make a Nation out of a People which distrusts itself. If we believe in ourselves - if each individual in our ranks believes in himself, we shall carry this policy to victory against all the forces that may be arrayed against us...

We go to build the Nation up from within, and we deny the right of any but our own countrymen to shape its course. That course is not England's and we shall not justify our course to England. The craven policy that has rotted our nation has been the policy of justifying our existence in our enemy's eyes. Our misfortunes are manifold but we are still men and women of a common family, and we owe no nation an apology for living in accordance with the laws of our being. In the British Liberal as in the British Tory we see our enemy, and in those who talk of ending British misgovernment we see the helots. It is not British misgovernment, but British government in Ireland, good or bad, we stand opposed to, and in that holy opposition we seek to band all our fellow-countrymen.

For the Orangeman of the North, ceasing to be the blind instrument of his own as well as his fellow-countrymen's destruction, we have the greeting of brotherhood as for the

Nationalist of the South, long taught to measure himself by English standards and save the face of tyranny by sending Irishmen to sit impotently in a foreign legislature whilst it forges the instruments of his oppression...

First resolutions adopted

Resolutions adopted at the meeting in the Rotunda on 28 November 1905.

That the people of Ireland are a free people, and that no law made without their authority or consent is or ever can be binding on their conscience. That the General Council of County Councils presents the nucleus of a national authority and we urge upon it, to extend the scope of its deliberation and action; to take within its purview every question of national interest and to formulate lines of procedure for the nation.

That National self-development through recognition of the duties and rights of citizenship on the part of the individual, and by the aid and support of all movements originating from within Ireland, instinct with National tradition, and not looking outside Ireland for the accomplishment of their aims, is vital to Ireland.

After the conference, which lasted most of the day, the first Sinn Féin public meeting was held that evening when the programme was presented to the large crowd which thronged the Rotunda Round Room. The meeting concluded with the singing of Thomas Davis's anthem, 'A Nation Once Again'.

The Dungannon Clubs

Bulmer Hobson and Denis McCullough, Belfast members of the secret revolutionary organisation, the Irish Republican Brotherhood, founded the openly separatist Dungannon Clubs in March 1905, the same year Sinn Féin emerged. Seán MacDiarmada of Leitrim, who had moved to Belfast, was a founder member. He was later a signatory of the 1916 Proclamation and executed for his part in the Easter Rising. The object of

A THING OF THE PAST.

JOHN REDMOND—"Bad luck to that infernal machine with the foreign name. Ever since it come on the road I have lost any fares I had. I can't afford to give the poor baste a feed of oats. I'm to blame meself. Me ould yoke is a bit slow, and it's out of date. I was wan time in comfortable circumstances."

Political cartoon

Members of Inghinidhe na hÉireann (Daughters of Erin), 1905-1906. Maud Gonne is centre, holding banner.

Sinn Féin Constitution, 1907

While the policy and name of Sinn Féin date from 1905, the formal organisation of the movement came about in August 1907 when Cumann na nGael, the National Council and the Dungannon Clubs amalgamated as Sinn Féin. The constitution adopted in 1907 reflected Griffith's concept of a dual monarchy but there was significant republican involvement through such key figures as Seán MacDiarmada.

The object of Sinn Féin is the reestablishment of the independence of Ireland.

The aim of the Sinn Féin Policy is to unite Ireland on this broad platform:

(1st) That we are a distinct nation.

(2nd) That we will not make any voluntary compact with Great Britain until Great Britain keeps her own compact which she made with the Renunciation Act of 1783, which enacted 'that the right claimed by the people of Ireland to be bound only by laws enacted by His Majesty and the Parliament of that Kingdom is hereby declared to be established and ascertained forever, and shall, at no time hereafter, be questioned or questionable'.

(3rd) That we are determined to make use of any powers we have, or may have at any time in the future, to work for our own advancement and for the creation of a prosperous, virile and independent nation.

Political cartoon

"I have come home to tell you the truth"
The first election

C.J. Dolan was elected MP for North Leitrim in 1906. Frustrated at the Irish Party's ineffectiveness in the Westminster Parliament, he resigned his seat and joined Sinn Féin, leading to a by-election in 1908. He was defeated at the polls by his former party but his 1,157 votes were the first cast for Sinn Féin in a parliamentary election and presaged the overwhelming victory a decade later. This is part of C.J. Dolan's election address published in the newspaper Sinn Féin in February 1908.

Two years ago you sent me to be your representative in the British House of Commons. You sent me to voice your demand for Self-Government, and you also gave me a mandate to strive for whatever remedial measures lay within our reach, and I went to the House of Commons determined to serve your interests and the interests of our country to the best of my ability. But I was not long there before I realised the truth of Michael Davitt's statement — that no Irish grievance, however genuine, would ever be remedied in that assembly unless the Government had to choose between reform and martial law in Ireland... The day of Parnell, Davitt and the Land League is over, and the voice of Ireland is drowned amidst contending English factions...

I have come home to tell you the truth, and to abide by the consequences; I have come to tell you that the Irish Members are helpless in the House of Commons, where they are outnumbered six to one, and their speeches are unheeded; that the proper place for the representatives of Ireland to meet is Dublin, not London; that the true field of action is Ireland, not England; that it is only by our efforts that Ireland can be raised to a position of prosperity and started on the path of national development; and that in appealing to Englishmen we are wasting our energies and demoralising our people...

I stand for Ireland, Free, Self-reliant and Prosperous... Sinn Féin means the end of empty talk and humbug, and the beginning of genuine National work; it means more wealth, more employment, and better wages for the people; it heralds the dawn of a new era rich with promise for our long suffering country, and as a believer in the policy of Sinn Féin, a believer in a self-reliant, self-supporting Ireland, I confidently solicit your support.

James Connolly on Griffith's Sinn Féin

The great Irish socialist republican and trade union leader, James Connolly, had worked with Griffith in anti-imperialist campaigns, including opposition to English royal visits and against British Army recruiting. This article was published in the Irish Nation *newspaper in January 1909:*

Sinn Féin has two sides — its economic teaching and its philosophy of self-reliance. With its economic teaching, as expounded by my friend Mr. Arthur Griffith in his adoption of the doctrines of Frederick List, Socialists have no sympathy, as it appeals only to those who measure a nation's prosperity by the volume of wealth produced in a country, instead of by the distribution of that wealth amongst the inhabitants. According to that

James Connolly

definition, Ireland in 1847 was a prosperous country because it exported food, whereas Denmark was comparatively unprosperous because it exported little.

But with that part of Sinn Féin which teaches that Ireland must rely upon itself, respect her own traditions know her own history, preserve her own language and literature without prejudice to, or denial of, the worth in the language and literature of other people, stand erect in her own worth and claim to be appraised for her own intrinsic value, and not as part of the wheels and cogs of the imperial system of another people — with that side of Sinn Féin Socialists may sympathise; and indeed, as a cold matter of fact, these doctrines were preached in Dublin by the Irish Socialist Republican Party from 1896 onward, before the Sinn Féin movement was founded...

Life in 'West Britain'

Sydney Gifford Czira was a Republican journalist and writer brought up in a wealthy middle-class family in Dublin. Here she describes the atmosphere around the time Sinn Féin was founded and when nationalists were attempting to revive a sense of Irish nationality. From her recollections 'The Years Flew By':

Our family home in Dublin was on the south side, in what was called a 'good residential district', which meant, in those days, a stronghold of British Imperialism. More than anything else the district resembled a waxworks museum. The people who surrounded us were lifelike but inanimate models of distinguished English people. It was a deadly atmosphere, in which any originality of thought or independence of action was regarded as eccentricity or lawlessness. You have guessed it! It was Rathmines: butt of local humour for a couple of generations because it residents seemed to typify the flunky Irishman; with their strange, synthetic English accent, their snobbery, and their half-hearted desire to be a ruling caste...

English history was taught as if it were a rubber stamp, to be pressed on your brain and give you a British trade mark — you learnt the dates when English kings reigned, fought battles and died. As for Irish history — whenever I hear anyone singing 'Who Fears to Speak of '98?' I feel that a great many of our generation could have answered that question by saying 'every single teacher in the school where I was taught'.

Sydney Gifford

It was a well-kept secret in my old school that we lived in Ireland, or had any history of our own at all. This school was typical of its day, and you would hardly believe the snobbery and social distinctions that existed among the children. I remember on my first day, being questioned by a group of other girls to make sure that I was of the right social standing before they would associate with me in any way. 'What is your father's profession? And where do you live? And where do you spend your holidays?' In those days, by the way, the question of where you spent your holidays was considered very important; it gave a clue as to your income. If you didn't go away to a select seaside resort in the summer you were poor — an unforgivable sin. Some people in good residential districts who couldn't afford to go away, used to pull down the blinds in the front of the house and retire into the back for the summer months...

The Police, having no useful employment, spend their time in country places sneaking round spying upon the people.

Political cartoon

The Irish Citizen Army paraded in front of Liberty Hall on the
outbreak of the First World War.

Birth of the Republic
1910-1918

Má fealltar orainn arís...

Bhí dhá olltoghchán Westminster i 1910 agus tar a éis bhí Rialtas Liobrálach i gcumhacht le tacaíocht ó Pháirtí na hÉireann faoi cheannas John Redmond. I 1912 foilsíodh an tríú Bhille Home Rule ag an Rialtas sin. Labhair Pádraig Mac Piarais ag cruinniú poiblí ollmhór i Sráid Uí Chonaill ar an 31 Márta 1912. Labhair Redmond ag an cruinniú céanna ach faoi dheireadh na bliana bhí an Piarsach ina bhall be Bhráithreachas na Poblachta.

Céard tá uainn? Ta saoirse Gael. Ní thigimíd ar fad le chéile i mion-nithe. Is cuma sin. Táimíd ar fad ar aon aigne i dtaobh na méide seo - go bhfuil de dhualgas orainn saoirse a bhaint amach dár gcine ar ais nó ar éigean. Tá dream dínn a bheadh sásta le bheith faoi cheannas Rí Shasana ach saoirse a bheith againn inar bhfearainn féin. Tá dream eile dínn nár chrom ár gceann is ná fheac ár nglúin in omós do Rí Shasana riamh agus nach ndéanfaidh go deo. Táim-se ar an dara den dá dhream sin mar is eol do chách...

Ach chítear dom gur amhlaidh bheinn ag déanamh feall ar mo mhuintir lá curtha an chatha muna bhfreagróinn an chomhghairm seo inniu óir is léir domsa go rachaidh an reacht seo atá dá mholadh dúinn i dtairbhe do Ghaeil agus go mba treise Gaeil chum troda `faoin reacht ná ina éagmais. An té atá ar an intinn sin ní bheadh ann ach cladhaire mura dtiúrfadh sé cúnamh chun an reacht a bhaint amach. Ná tuigtear go bhfuilim ag glacadh leis an reacht roimh ré. Níl éinne ag glacadh leis an reacht roimh ré. B'fhéidir go mbeadh orainn diúltú don reacht. Níl dá rá againn inniu ach go gcaifear éisteacht le glór Gael feasta, go bhfuil ár bhfoighid caite.

Tá Gaeil dá fhógairt agus dhá chéad míle díobh ag labhairt anseo d'aitheasc aonduine go bhfuil saoirse uatha agus go bhfuil fúthu a bhaint amach. Cuirimís le chéile agus bainimís racht maith de Ghaill. Is dóigh liom gur féidir reacht maith a bhaint díobh ach ár ndóthain misnigh do ghabháil chugainn. Agus má clistear orainn den dul seo tá dream in Éirinn agus táimse ar dhuine díobh a mholfas do Ghaeil gan dul i gcomhairle le Gaill go deo arís ach iad a fhreagairt le lámh láidir agus le faobhar claidhimh. Tuigeadh Gaill má fealltar orainn arís go mbeidh ina chogadh chraorag ar fud na hÉireann.

Roger Casement on Tory/Unionist reaction

Encouraged and aided by the Tory Party in Britain, the Unionist Party in Ireland rallied behind Edward Carson and James Craig to oppose Home Rule. Their 'Solemn League and Covenant' was signed by thousands of their supporters in 1912. Roger Casement, member of the British diplomatic service and internationally acclaimed for humanitarian work in Africa and South America, was also a County Antrim Protestant, a fervent Irish nationalist and early supporter of Sinn Féin. He writes to his cousin about the Unionists:

Roger Casement

How appalling they look with their grim Ulster Hall faces, all going down to curse the Pope and damn Home Rule in kirk and meeting house, and let their God out for one day of the week — poor old Man, with his teeth broke with the cursing. I presume you read the Covenant? You see He is trotted out there. They are confident He will 'defend the Right'. Supposing he doesn't! How awful if God should turn out to be a disloyalist!...

The poor duped, sincere multitude of honest boys has paraded before Carson, Smith and the God of our Fathers... I love the Antrim Presbyterians - Antrim and Down - they are good, kind, warm-hearted souls — and to see them now exploited, by that damned Church of Ireland — that Orange ascendancy gang who hate Presbyterians only less than Papishes, and to see them delirious before a Smith, a Carson (a cross between a badly raised bloodhound and an underfed hyena, sniffing for Irish blood in the track) and whooping 'Rule Britannia' through the streets, is a wound to my soul. For they are Irish right through, really.

Principles of Freedom

The newspaper Irish Freedom *was established by the Irish Republican Brotherhood, which had been reorganised by Seán MacDiarmada and Tom Clarke. It ran from 1910 to 1915 and one its most talented and thoughtful contributors was Traolach Mac Suibhne (Terence MacSwiney). He wrote a series of articles entitled 'Principles of Freedom', published in book form in 1921. While many supporters of Home Rule looked forward to Ireland*

Traolach Mac Suibhne

gaining a profitable share in the British Empire, Irish Republicans like Mac Suibhne were anti-imperialists and sympathised with other oppressed peoples of the Empire.

That we shall win our freedom I have no doubt; that we shall use it well I am not so certain, for see how sadly misused it is abroad though the world today. That should be our final consideration, and we should make this a resolution — our future history shall be more glorious than that of any contemporary state. We shall look for prosperity, no doubt, but let our enthusiasm be for beautiful living; we shall build up our strength, yet not for conquest, but as a pledge of brotherhood and a defence for the weaker ones of the earth; we shall take pride in our institutions, not only as guaranteeing the stability of the state, but as securing the happiness of the citizens, and we shall lead Europe again as we led it of old. We shall rouse the world from the wicked dream of material greed, of tyrannical power, of corrupt and callous politics to the wonder of a regenerated spirit, a new and beautiful dream; and we shall establish our state in a true freedom that will endure forever...

With the immediate promise of Home Rule many strange apologists for the Empire have stepped into the sun. Perhaps it is well — we may find ourselves soon more directly than heretofore struggling with the Empire. So far the fight has been confused. Imperialists fighting for Home Rule obscured the fact that they were not fighting the Empire. Now Home Rule is likely to come, and it will serve at least the good purpose of clearing the air and setting the issue definitely between the nation and the Empire. We shall have our say for the nation, but as even now many things, false and hypocritical, are being urged on behalf of the Empire, it will serve us to examine the Imperial creed and show its tyranny, cruelty, hypocrisy, and expose the danger of giving it any pretext whatever for aggression. For the Empire as we know it and deal with it is a bad thing in itself, and we must not only get free of it and not again be trapped by it, but must rather give hope and encouragement to every nation fighting the same fight the world over...

If Ireland is to be regenerated we must have internal unity; if the world is to be regenerated we must have worldwide unity, not of government but of brotherhood. To this great end every individual, every nation, has a duty; and that the end may not be missed we must continually turn for the correction of our philosophy to reflecting on the common origin of the human race, on the beauty of the world that is the heritage of all, our common hopes and fears, and in the greatest sense the mutual interests of the peoples of the earth.

The Great Lockout, 1913

Thousands of Dublin workers were locked out by their employers when they refused to sign a pledge not to join the Irish Transport and General Workers' Union (ITGWU). In the Irish Worker *on 30 August, James Connolly described the background to the Lockout:*

Dublin Metropolitan Police baton charge strikers during the Lockout.

Inset: Arrest of Jim Larkin

The Irish Transport and General Workers' Union found that before its advent the working class of Dublin had been taught by all the educational agencies of the country, by all the social influences of their masters, that this world was created for the special benefit of the various sections of the master class, that kings and lords and capitalists were of value; that even flunkeys, toadies, lickspittles and poodle dogs had an honoured place in the scheme of the universe, but that there was neither honour, credit nor consideration to the man or woman who toils to maintain them all.

Freedom's Martyrs

Members of the Irish Women Workers Union who suffered terms of imprisonment in the cause of Labour

Members of the Irish Women Workers Union who played a key role in the 1913 lockout.

Against all this the Irish Transport and General Workers' Union has taught that they who toil are the only ones that do matter, that all others are but beggars upon the bounty of those who work with hand or brain, and that this superiority of social value can at any time be realised, be translated into actual fact, by the combination of the labouring class. Preaching, organising, and fighting upon this basis, the Irish Transport and General Workers' Union found Dublin the poorest city in these countries by reason of its lack of these qualities. And by imbuing the workers with them, it has made Dublin the richest city in Europe to-day, rich by all that counts for greatness in the history of nations.

It is then upon the working class so enslaved, this working class so led and so enriched with moral purposes and high aims that the employers propose to make general war. Shall we shrink from it; cower before their onset? A thousand times no! Shall we crawl back into our slums, abase our hearts, bow our knees, and crawl once more to lick the hand that would smite us? Shall we, who have been carving out for our children a brighter future, a cleaner city, a freer life, consent to betray them instead into the grasp of the blood-suckers from whom we have dreamt of escaping? No, no and yet again no! Let them declare their lock-out; it will only hasten the day when the working class will lock-out the capitalist class for good and all.

Sinn Féin, Republicans and the Lockout

Arthur Griffith, while he remained on civil terms with James Connolly, opposed Jim Larkin in his newspaper and denounced his leadership of the Dublin workers. But Griffith's opposition to the ITGWU was not shared by everyone in Sinn Féin, many of whose members were trade unionists. Such Dublin labour leaders as P.T. Daly, William Partridge and Michael O'Lehane had been early members and councillors for Sinn Féin on Dublin City Council. Prominent Republicans, such as those quoted below, sided with the workers in their struggle.

Constance Markievicz

Sitting there listening to Larkin I realised that I was in the presence of something that I had never come across before, some great primeval force of nature rather than a man. A tornado, a storm-driven wave, the rush into life of spring, and the blasting breath of autumn, all seemed to emanate from the power that spoke. It seemed as if his personality caught up, assimilated and threw back to the vast crowd that surrounded him every emotion that swayed them, every pain and joy that they had ever felt made articulate and sanctified. Only the great elemental force that is in all crowds had passed into his nature forever... this force of his magically changed the whole life of the workers in Dublin and the whole outlook of trade unionism in Ireland.

Pádraig Mac Piarais

My instinct is with the landless men against the lord of lands, and with the breadless man against the master of millions. I may be wrong but I hold it a most terrible sin that there should be landless men in this island of waste yet fertile valleys, and that there should be breadless men in this city where great fortunes are made and enjoyed...

I calculate that one third of the people of Dublin are under-fed; that half the children attending Irish primary schools are ill-nourished. Inspectors of the National Board will tell you that there is no use in visiting primary schools in Ireland after one or two in the afternoon: the children are too weak and drowsy with hunger to be capable of answering intelligently. I suppose there are 20,000 families in Dublin in whose domestic economy milk and butter are all but unknown: black tea and dry bread are their staple articles of diet. There are many thousand fireless hearth-places in Dublin on the bitterest days of winter; there would be many thousand more only for such bodies as the Society of St. Vincent de Paul. 20,000 Dublin families live in one-room tenements. It is common to find two or three families occupying the same room; and sometimes one of the families will have a lodger. There are tenement rooms in Dublin where over a dozen persons live, eat and sleep...

I do not know whether the methods of Mr. James Larkin are wise methods or unwise methods (unwise, I think, in some respects) but this I know, that here is a most hideous wrong to be righted and that the man who attempts to right it is a good and a brave man.

Thomas Ashe

Letter to his brother, Gregory Ashe, in the USA.

I suppose you know by this that Jem Larkin was sent to jail. He's out for the last two or three days again. The government got afraid of a general strike in England which the Englishmen were organising in his favour. So they let him out. He and Jem Connolly are now asking their men to drill like Carson's. If we had them all drilled I know what they'd direct their rifles on very soon. I hope they'll continue drilling. We are all here on Larkin's side. He'll beat hell out of the snobbish, mean, seoinín employers yet, and more power to him.

Irish Citizen Army on the roof of Liberty Hall, overlooking Butt Bridge

The Irish Citizen Army

Workers and their families were subjected to widespread brutality from the police and the hired thugs of the employers during the Great Lockout. Their response was to establish the Irish Citizen Army which was announced by James Connolly in October 1913. Frank Robbins remembers:

One night during October 1913 I attended a meeting in Beresford Place and heard Connolly, speaking from the central window of Liberty Hall, say that as a result of the brutalities of the Royal Irish Constabulary and the Dublin Metropolitan Police, it was intended to organise and discipline a force to protect workers' meetings and to prevent such activities — by armed thugs — occurring in the future. This was the first open declaration I heard regarding the formation of the Irish Citizen Army. It was my intention to become a member of that that army and I awaited with interest the first step to be taken...

Without Connolly in Dublin the Irish Citizen Army would probably have dithered itself out of existence. The necessary contact between Connolly and Pearse, Clarke and McDermott and between Dublin and Belfast would have been very difficult and probably so intermittent that plans would have been impossible to complete.

Shortly after Connolly took charge Thomas Foran briefed him on how to get the support of the Dublin working class. "If you want to get on in this city," he told him, "you'll have to give a whole lot of moonshine talk. This is what they've been used to and it's the only way."

Connolly's reply to this advice shows a basic difference between him and Larkin. "If you or anybody else expect," he said, "that I'm going to waste my time talking 'bosh' to the crowds in Beresford Place, for the sake of hearing shouts — then you'll be sadly disappointed. I would rather give my message to four serious-minded men at any cross-roads in Ireland and know that they would carry it back to the places they came from and that it would fall on fertile ground and bear fruit in the future."

Óglaigh na hÉireann — the Irish Volunteers

The Ulster Volunteer Force was established in January 1913 to resist Home Rule. They were assisted with arms, training and officers by the Tory Party in England who were using the Home Rule crisis to oppose the Liberal government. In September, the Unionists established a 'Provisional Government of Ulster' under Carson and demanded that the nine counties of Ulster be excluded from the Home Rule Bill. The IRB had already decided that the Irish Volunteers should be established and the opportunity came when the academic and Conradh na Gaeilge activist, Eoin MacNeill, wrote an article entitled 'The North Began', urging that the Ulster Volunteers' example be followed. After an initial organising meeting in Wynn's Hotel on 11th November 1913, Óglaigh na hÉireann was established in the Rotunda — also the birthplace of Sinn Féin — at a public rally on 25 November. Seán T. Ó Ceallaigh, then a prominent member of Sinn Féin, recalls the occasion:

I well remember Tom Clarke rubbing his hands with glee when speaking about the reports of Ulster Volunteer activity. "Let them fire away, the more they organise the better," he would say. "Aren't they setting us a splendid example? Soon, very soon, we will be following in their footsteps. But let us take our time. Don't let us act hastily. We must see to it that the first step is taken by the right people. We — that is the IRB — should not show our hand too early... Oh lads, the day is coming and is coming quickly when boys all over Ireland will be drilling and marching and, maybe, learning the use of arms too. Won't that be a great day for Ireland, boys?" he would say to one or two of us to whom he knew he could talk freely, as he stood behind his counter in Parnell Street...

Eventually the day came to bring the Volunteers into existence. The announcement that a meeting was to be held in the Rink, Rotunda Gardens, to found an Irish Volunteer organisation aroused the greatest enthusiasm. The fact that it was Eoin MacNeill who invited the men of Dublin to come in their thousands and join the Volunteers seemed to give universal satisfaction. This call came at a time when, almost daily, Dublin was full of excitement. Thousands of Dublin workers, dockers, tramway men and others had been on strike for months. Workers and police were in almost daily conflict. Captain White, son of a British general famed for his defence of Ladysmith, South Africa, in the Boer War, who sided with the workers, had recently proposed the formation of a Citizen Army to defend the workers in their giant struggle for justice.

All this added to the excitement of the night of 25 November, when the men of Dublin came in their thousands to join and help Eoin MacNeill and his provisional committee in setting up the Irish Volunteers to defend Home Rule. I am not sure how many that building, the Rotunda Rink, could hold, maybe three thousand. But many more came to attend the meeting...

Manifesto of the Irish Volunteers, 25 November 1913

At a time when legislative proposals universally confessed to be of vital concern for the future of Ireland have been put forward, and are awaiting decision, a plan has been deliberately adopted by one of the great English political parties, advocated by the leaders of that party and by its numerous organs in the Press, and brought systematically to bear on English public opinion, to make the display of military force and the menace of armed violence the determining factor in the future relations between this country and Great Britain.

The party which has thus substituted open force for the semblance of civil government is seeking by this means not merely to decide an immediate political

Irish Volunteers Poster

OBJECTS OF THE IRISH VOLUNTEERS.

1. To secure and maintain the rights and liberties common to the people of Ireland.

2. To train, discipline, and equip for this purpose an Irish Volunteer Force.

3. To unite, in the service of Ireland, Irishmen of every creed, and of every party and class.

Oglaiġ na hÉireann
(The Irish Volunteers)

No. 02667

Membership Card

Irish Volunteers Membership Card

issue of grave concern to this Nation, but also to obtain for itself the future control of all our national affairs. It is plain to every man that the people of Ireland, if they acquiesce in this new policy by their inaction, will consent to the surrender, not only of their rights as a nation, but of their civic rights as men.

Are we to rest inactive, in the hope that the course of politics in Great Britain may save us from the degradation openly threatened against us? British politics are controlled by British interests, and are complicated by problems of great importance to the people of Great Britain. In a crisis of this kind, the duty of safeguarding our own rights is our duty first and foremost. They have rights who dare maintain them. If we remain quiescent, by what title can we expect the people of Great Britain to turn aside from their own pressing concerns to defend us? Will not such an attitude of itself mark us out as a people unworthy of defence.

Such is the occasion, not altogether unfortunate, which has brought about the inception of the Irish Volunteer movement. But the Volunteers, once they have been enrolled, will form a prominent element in the national life under a National government. The Nation will maintain its Volunteer organisation as a guarantee of the liberties which the Irish people shall have secured...

The object proposed for the Irish Volunteers is to secure and maintain the rights and liberties common to all the people of Ireland. Their duties will be defensive and protective, and they will not contemplate either aggression or domination. Their ranks are open to all able-bodied Irishmen without distinction of creed, politics or social grade...

A proportion of time spared, not from work, but from pleasure and recreation, a voluntary adoption of discipline, a purpose firmly and steadily carried through, will renew the vitality of the Nation. Even that degree of self-discipline will bring back to every town, village and countryside a consciousness that has long been forbidden them — the sense of freemen who have fitted themselves to defend the cause of freedom...

Members of Cumann na mBan, 1921

Inset right: Cumann na mBan Constitution

Inset below: Women who took part in the Easter Rising, pictured in Dublin, in the summer of 1916

CONSTITUTION, CORUGHADH.

Cumann na mBan is an independent body of Irishwomen pledged to maintain the Irish Republic established on January 21st, 1919, and to organise and train the women of Ireland to work unceasingly for its international ... ...men of Irish birth or descent are eligible for membership, ... an who is a member of the enemy organisation or who ... e Government of the Republic as the lawfully constituted ... people can become a member.

...spora)

...mplete separation of Ireland from all foreign powers.
...ity of Ireland.
...elicisation of Ireland.

...(Slighthe).

... the Republic by every means in our power against all ... domestic.

...glaigh na h-Eireann, the Irish Volunteers, in its fight to ...lic.

...ctions, Cumann na mBan, as such, give no assistance to ...hich does not give allegiance to the Government of the

...perfect citizens of a perfect Irish Nation by :—
... Honour, Truth, Courage and Temperance as the watch-
...mBan ; (b) by fostering an Irish atmosphere, politically,
...ocially ; (c) discouraging Emigration by brightening the
...rict ; (d) supporting Irish industries.

... and in all places to uphold the spirit and the letter of the
...onstitution.

...ution of Cumann na mBan may not be altered except by a two-third majority vote of a Convention.

The spawning of Partition

The English Liberal government of Prime Minister Herbert Asquith backed down before Tory/Unionist threats of violence and spawned the Partition of Ireland. When the Home Rule Bill had its second reading for its last session in the House of Commons in March 1914, Asquith proposed 'county option with a time limit' by which any Ulster county might vote itself out of Home Rule for a period of six years. Seeing that they had the Liberals and John Redmond on the run, Carson and the Tory/Unionists pushed further. When the Liberal government made preparations for the British Army to strengthen its garrison in Ulster, its Commander-in-Chief in Ireland, General Sir Arthur Paget, would not move troops and 57 officers at the Curragh said they would prefer to accept dismissal if ordered North. The Curragh Mutiny and the first move to partition the country struck Ireland like a thunderbolt. It was James Connolly who saw most clearly what Partition would mean, as is clear from his writings in March 1914:

The recent proposals of Messrs. Asquith, Devlin, Redmond and Co. for the settlement of the Home Rule question... reveal in a most striking and unmistakable manner the depth of betrayal to which the so-called Nationalist politicians are willing to sink... It is the trusted leaders of Ireland that in secret conclave with the enemies of Ireland have agreed to see Ireland as a nation disrupted politically and her children divided under separate political governments with warring interests.

Funeral of victims of Bacherlor's Walk shootings by the British Army, July 1914

38

Now, what is the position of Labour towards it all? Let us remember that the Orange aristocracy now fighting for its supremacy in Ireland has at all times been based upon a denial of the common human rights of the Irish people; that the Orange Order was not founded to safeguard religious freedom, but to deny religious freedom, and that it raised this religious question, not for the sake of any religion, but in order to use religious zeal in the interests of the oppressive property rights of rackrenting landlords and sweating capitalists. That the Irish people might be kept asunder and robbed whilst so sundered and divided, the Orange aristocracy went down to the lowest depths and out of the lowest pits of hell brought up the abominations of sectarian feuds to stir the passions of the ignorant mob. No crime was too brutal or cowardly; no lie too base; no slander too ghastly, as long as they served to keep the democracy asunder...

And lo and behold, the trusted guardians of the people, the vaunted saviours of the Irish race, agree in front of the enemy and in face of the world to sacrifice to the bigoted enemy the unity of the nation, and along with it the lives, liberties and hopes of that portion of the nation which in the midst of the most hostile surroundings have fought to keep the faith in things national and progressive.

Such a scheme as that agreed by Redmond and Devlin, the betrayal of the national democracy of industrial Ulster, would mean a carnival of reaction both North and South, would set back the wheels of progress, would destroy the oncoming unity of the Irish Labour movement and paralyse all advanced movements whilst it endured.

To it Labour should give the bitterest opposition, against it Labour in Ulster should fight even to the death, if necessary, as our fathers fought before us...

Belfast is bad enough as it is; what it would be under such rule the wildest imagination cannot conceive. Filled with the belief that they were defeating the Imperial Government and the Nationalists combined, the Orangemen would have scant regards for the rights of the minority left at their mercy....

Fianna Éireann leis na gunnaí ag cuan Bhinn Éadair

Gunnaí Bhinn Éadair

I mí Aibreán 1914 thóg an UVF 35,000 raidhfil agus armlón isteach sa tír. Níor chuir Arm na Breataine na Constáblacht Ríoga na hÉireann bac leo. I mi Iúil na bliana sin tháinig captaen an long Asgard, Erskine Childers, isteach i gcuan Bhinn Éadair le 900 raidhfil Mauser ar son Óglaigh na hÉireann. Scaoil Arm na Breataine ar an bpobal i lár na cathrach níos déanaí an lá sin agus maraíodh triúr. Bhí Séamus Ó Maoileoin ina Óglach ag Binn Éadair.

I mí Iúil 1914 a tháinig na gunnaí go Beann Éadair agus bhí na hÓglaigh ina saighdiúirí feasta. Deineann mothú an ghunna ina láimh nó ar a ghualainn níos mo chun spiorad an tsaighdiúra a mhúscailt sa duine ná blianta fada ag léamh agus ag foghliaim agus ag cleachtadh na ceirde...Nach orm a bhí an t-áthas agus mé ag máirseáil go Beann Éadair an lá sin! Bheadh an gunna a gheall Liam o Maoilíosa dom trí bliana roimhe sin ar mo ghualainn agam agus me ag filleadh abhaile. Bhí daoine ann an lá sin nach raibh fhios acu go raibh gunnaí ag teacht ach bhí gach duine ar bior ag súil le heacht. Bhí tintreach san aer.

B'shin í an chéad uair a leag me súil ar Éamon de Valéra. Bhí sé mar chaptaen ar an mbuíon ina raibh mise. Fir ón tuaith is mó a bhí sa bhuíon sin agus ní raibh aithne againn air. Bhí mé díreach taobh thiar de agus bhí mo chroí briste ag iarraidh siúl i gcomhchéim leis.

"Cé hé an fathach?" arsa firín as Cúige Uladh a bhi le m'ais.

"Ní fhaca mé riamh roimhe seo e," arsa mise.

"Oifigeach Spáinneach is ea é atá ag múineadh saighdiúreachtas do mhuintir Bhleá Cliath," arsa an tríú fear.

"Cá bhfuair sé an Ghaeilge?" arsa mise, mar bhí na horduithe aige as Ghaeilge.

"Chaith sé seachtain i gConamara agus rug bean abhaile leis a mhúin an Ghaeilge dó."

"Níor chuir sé aon am amú ann" arsa an tUltach.

Bhí an long sa chuan nuair a shroich muid Caladh Bheann Éadair. Thosaigh díluchtú láithreach. Sheas muid i gceithre línte faid an chalaidh agus síneadh na gunnaí ó dhuine go duine. Níor tugadh aon philéir dúinn go fóill, ar eagla na timpiste is dócha. Ní fios dom cé mhéid fear a bhi ann. Ocht gcéad b'fhéidir. Cuireadh roinnt gunnaí ar loraithe leis agus boscaí piléar. Bhí roinnt bleachtairí ann ach níor tugadh cead dóibh teacht ar an gcaladh. Thug muid aghaidh ar an gcathair láithreach.

Tháníg muid slán chomh fada le Cluain Tarbh, áit a raibh seisear píléir déag agus complacht saighdiúirí romhainn. Thug Liam Ó MaoilÍosa ordú do na céad cheithre línte síneadh trasna an bhóthair. Dhein na píléirí iarracht ar na gunnaí a thógáil uainn. Bhí raic ann ar feadh cúpla nóiméad, gunnaí folmha ar thoabh amháin agus bataí píléirí ar an taobh eile. Níor ghlac na saighdiúirí aon pháirt, ach beirt nó triúr a thánig i gcabhair ar philéirí a leagadh. Gortaíodh roinnt ar an dá thaobh. Fuair mise buille bata ar an ngualainn...

Molly Childers and Mary Spring Rice on board the Asgard

Thóg muid ceithre cinn an duine. Aon duine a d'iompair 'gunna Bheann Éadair', mar a tugtaí orthu, riamh, tá fhios aige go raibh ualach orainn. Shroich muid faiche Mhainistir Mharino. D'fhág muid na gunnaí ansin agus ceathrar seanbhráthar ina mbun agus d'fhill muid ag bailiú tuilleadh. Nuair shroich muid Marino athuair bhí na bráithre ag seasamh garda ar na gunnaí agus gunnaí ar a nguaillí acu. Is mór an trua nach raibh camera agam. Bhí duine amháin a bhí os cionn ochtó ma bhí sé lá agus é chomh díreach le ribe ag siúl suas agus anuas mar dhea gur shaighdiúir é.

Sinn Féin urges Irish neutrality in the War

The Quiz

HARVESTER: "Any work to-day, Pat?"
PAT: "No, Con; go back and tell Northcliffe and Company they sent you here on a fool's errand."
[At numerous public meetings throughout the country resolutions have been carried unanimously
denouncing any attempt to introduce Conscription into Ireland.]

6.3 'On the Road'. (*Quiz*, October 1915)

Political Cartoon

On the outbreak of the Great War, John Redmond, who had imposed his nominees onto the Provisional Committee of the Irish Volunteers, pledged the Volunteers to defend Ireland for the British government, and then to fight wherever they were sent. From the first, Sinn Féin was vehemently opposed to Irish participation in the war. This editorial is from Sinn Féin, 8 August 1914.

Ireland is not at war with Germany. She has no quarrel with any Continental Power. England is at war with Germany, and Mr. Redmond has offered England the services of the National Volunteers to 'defend Ireland'. What has Ireland to defend and whom has she to defend it against? Has she a native Constitution or a National Government to defend? All know she has not. All know both were wrested from her by the power to whom Mr. Redmond offers the services of Nationalist Ireland. All know that Mr. Redmond has made his offer without receiving a quid pro quo. There is no European power waging war against the people of Ireland. There are two European Powers at war with the people who dominate Ireland from Dublin Castle. The call to the Volunteers to 'defend Ireland' is a call to them to defend the bureaucracy entrenched in that edifice...

Our duty is in no doubt. We are Irish Nationalists and the only duty we can have is to stand for Ireland's interest, irrespective of the interests of England or Germany or any other foreign country...

The Funeral of Jeremiah O'Donovan Rossa

On 1 August 1915, the Irish Volunteers and the Irish Citizen Army, Fianna Éireann and Cumann na mBan joined forces for the funeral in Dublin of Jeremiah O'Donovan Rossa, the Fenian veteran who had died in America. The funeral, with its huge attendance and expertly martialled cortège, was a prelude to the 1916 Rising. The oration was delivered by Pádraig Mac Piarais.

A Ghaela,

Do hiarradh orm-sa labhairt inniu ar son a bhfuil cruinnuithe ar an láthair so agus ar son a bhfuil beo de Chlannaibh Gaedheal, ag moladh an leon do leagamar i gcré anseo agus ag gríosadh meanman na gcarad atá go brónach ina dhiaidh.

A chairde, ná bíodh brón ar éinne atá ina sheasamh ag an uaigh so, ach bíodh buíochas againn inár gcroíthe do Dhia na ngrás do chruthuigh anam uasal áluinn Dhiarmuda Uí Dhonnabháinn Rosa agus thug ré fhada dhó ar an saol so.

Ba chalma an fear thú, a Dhiarmuid. Is tréan d'fhearais cath ar son cirt do chine, is ní beag ar fhuilingis, agus ní dhéanfaidh Gaeil dearmad ort go bráth na breithe.

Ach, a chairde, na bíodh brón orainn, acht bíodh misneach inár gcroíthe agus bíodh neart inar gcuisleannaibh, óir cuimhnighimís nach mbíonn aon bhás ann nach mbíonn aiséirí ina dhiaidh, agus gurab as an uaigh so agus as na huaigheanna atá inár dtimcheall éireóchas saoirse Ghaedheal.

It has seemed right, before we turn away from this place in which we have laid the mortal remains of O'Donovan Rossa, that one among us should, in the name of all, speak the praise of that valiant man, and endeavor to formulate the thoughts and the hope that there are in us, as we stand around his grave. And if there is anything that makes it fitting that I rather than some other, I rather than one of the grey-haired men who were young with him and shared in his labour and suffering, should speak here, it is perhaps that I may be taken as speaking on behalf of a new generation that has been rebaptised in the Fenian faith, and that has accepted the responsibility of carrying out the Fenian programme.

I propose to you then that, here, by the grave of this unrepentant Fenian, we renew our baptismal vows; that, here by the grave of this unconquered and unconquerable man, we ask of God, each one for himself, such unshakable purpose, such high and gallant courage, such unbreakable strength of soul as belonged to O'Donovan Rossa.

Deliberately here we avow ourselves, as he avowed himself in the dock, Irishmen of one allegiance only. We of the Irish Volunteers, and you others who are associated with us in today's task and duty, are bound together and must stand together henceforth in brotherly union for the achievement of the freedom of Ireland. And we know only one definition of freedom; it is Tone's definition; it is Mitchel's definition. It is Rossa's definition. Let no man blaspheme the cause that the dead generations of Ireland served by giving it any other name and definition than their name and their definition.

We stand at Rossa's grave not in sadness but rather in exaltation of spirit that is has been given to us to come thus into so close a communion with that brave and splendid Gael. Splendid and holy causes are served by men who are themselves splendid and holy. O'Donovan Rossa was splendid in the proud manhood of him, splendid in the heroic grace of him, splendid in the Gaelic strength and clarity and truth of him. And all that splendour and pride and strength was compatible with a humility and a simplicity of devotion to Ireland, to all that was olden and beautiful and Gaelic in Ireland, the holiness and simplicity of patriotism of a Michael O'Clery or of an Eoghan O'Growney. The clear, true eyes of this man almost alone in his day visioned Ireland as we of today would surely have her; not free merely, but Gaelic as well: not Gaelic merely, but free as well.

In a closer spiritual communion with him now than ever before or perhaps ever again, in spiritual communion with those of his day, living and dead, who suffered with him in English prisons, in communion of spirit too with our own dear comrades, who suffer in

English prisons today, and speaking on their behalf as well as our own, we pledge to Ireland our love, and we pledge to English rule in Ireland our hate.

This is a place of peace, sacred to the dead, where men should speak with all charity and all restraint; but I hold it a Christian thing, as O'Donovan Rossa held it, to hate evil, to hate untruth, to hate oppression, and, hating them, to strive to overthrow them. Our foes are strong and wise and wary; but, strong and wise and wary as they are, they cannot undo the miracles of God who ripens in the hearts of young men the seeds sown by the young men of '65 and '67 are coming to their miraculous ripening today. Rulers and defenders of Realms had need to be wary if they would guard against such processes.

Life springs from death; and from the graves of patriot men and women spring living nations. The Defenders of this Realm have worked well in secret and in the open. They think that they have pacified Ireland. They think that they have pacified half of us and intimidated the other half. They think that they have foreseen everything, think that they have provided against everything; but the fools, the fools, the fools! — they have left us our Fenian dead — And while Ireland holds these graves, Ireland unfree shall never be at peace.

Cannon fodder for the Empire

One of the principal recruiters for the British Army in Ireland was Joe Devlin, Irish Party MP for West Belfast and head of the Ancient Order of Hibernians. In his paper, Worker's Republic, *on 28 August 1915, James Connolly wrote of 'Wee Joe Devlin':*

Belfast opponents of Joe Devlin usually refer to him sarcastically as the 'Wee Bottlewasher', alluding to his position before he climbed into power. The sarcasm is pointless. A bottlewasher was an honest occupation, but a recruiting sergeant luring to their death the men who trusted him and voted him into power is — ah, let us remember the Defence of the Realm Act.

The present writer cannot ride up the Falls Road in his own motor car, the penny tram has to do him. But thank God, there are no fresh made graves in Flanders or the Dardanelles filled by the mangled corpses of men whom he coaxed into leaving their homes and families.

Let me, who have led them into this, speak in my own and in my fellow-commanders' names and in the name of Ireland present and to come, their praise, and ask those who come after to remember them.

For four days they have fought, and toiled, almost without cessation, almost without sleep, and in the intervals of fighting, they have sung songs of the freedom of Ireland. No man has complained, no man has asked "why?" Each individual has spent himself, happy to pour out his strength for Ireland and for freedom. If they do not win this fight, at least they will have deserved to win it. But win it they will, although they may win it in death. Already they have won a great thing. They have redeemed Dublin from many shames, and made her name splendid among the names of cities.

If I were to mention names of individuals my list would be a long one.

I will name only that of Commandant General James Connolly, Commanding the Dublin division. He lies wounded, but is still the guiding brain of our resistance.

If we accomplish no more than we have accomplished I am satisfied that we have saved Ireland's honour. I am satisfied that we should have accomplished more, and we should have accomplished the task of enthroning, as well as proclaiming, the Irish Republic as a Sovereign state, had our arrangements for a simultaneous rising of the whole country, with a combined plan as sound as the Dublin plan has been proved to be, been allowed to go through on Easter Sunday. Of the fatal countermanding order which prevented these plans from being carried out, I shall not speak further. Both Eoin MacNeill and we have acted in the best interests of Ireland.

For my part, as to anything I have done in this, I am not afraid to face either the judgement of God, or the judgement of posterity.

P.H. Pearse
Commandant-General,
Commander-in-Chief, the Army of the Irish Republic
and President of the Provisional Government.

Tom Clarke's Message to the Irish People

I and my fellow signatories believe we have struck the first successful blow for Freedom. The next blow, which we have no doubt Ireland will strike, will win through. In this belief we die happy.

Thomas J. Clarke
Kilmainham Jail, 3 May, 1916.

Constance Markievicz (second from right) with Michael Mallin (later executed) under British Army guard after surrender

Last statement of Thomas MacDonagh

I, Thomas MacDonagh, having now heard the sentence of the Court Martial held on me today, declare that in all my acts — all the acts for which I have been arraigned — I have been actuated by one motive only, the love of my country, the desire to make her a sovereign independent state. I still hope and pray that my acts may have for consummation her lasting freedom and happiness.

I am to die at dawn, 3.30am 3rd May. I am ready to die, and I thank God that I die in so holy a cause. My country will reward my deed richly...

Cead Mile Fáilte

Constance Markievicz is greeted by thousands of people in Dublin on her release from prison in England

(inset): Cumann na mBan unit, 1916

The Election of the Snows

Geraldine Plunkett Dillon was the sister of Joseph Mary Plunkett, signatory of the Proclamation and executed 1916 leader. Here Geraldine describes the North Roscommon by-election of February 1917 which was won by her father, George Noble Count Plunkett. It was the first electoral test of public opinion after the Rising and Sinn Féin went on to win three more by-election victories in 1917 — in South Longford, East Clare and Kilkenny City.

Count Plunkett

The Irish Parliamentary Party took a victory for granted, especially as a very heavy fall of snow for many days before polling day seemed as if it would keep the country folk from the polling stations. But Father O'Flanagan organised teams of farmers who dug lanes through six-foot drifts and made passages for the cars to pass...

As well as the obstacle of the weather the organisers were hampered by having only three weeks in which to canvass votes; procure speakers at meetings; impersonation officers for the day of the election; and arrange transport to bring the candidate around the constituency. But everyone worked with the greatest willingness, and, in spite of the arctic conditions, there was the usual speech-making at meetings. Wherever the Sinn Féin candidate went scenes of enthusiasm were witnessed. The Volunteers were present at the polling stations on the Saturday of the election and after the booths closed they joined the local Royal Irish Constabulary in keeping guard over the ballot boxes from the Saturday evening until Monday morning when the count began...

My father was elected on 3 February and polled 3,022 votes... The excited enthusiasm over the victory was almost unprecedented. The people in sympathy with Sinn Féin were experiencing a sensation new to people of that time; it was success — a new kind of victory — for them, for Ireland. The Party followers were stunned and took their beating badly...

My father... later addressed his followers outside the courthouse in Boyle where the votes had been counted: "My place henceforth," he said, "will be beside you in your own country, for it is in Ireland with the people of Ireland, that the battle for Irish liberty will be fought. I recognise no Parliament in existence as

Geraldine Plunkett Dillon

having a right over the people of Ireland, just as I deny the right of England to one inch of the soil of Ireland. I do not think I will go further than the old house in College Green to represent you. I am sent by Ireland to represent you in Ireland; to stand by you and to win Ireland's freedom on her own soil."

This Sinn Féin success in the North Roscommon constituency was a prelude to three other election victories for the abstentionist policy in 1917 and these popular, much publicised events contributed in no small degree to reawakening of Ireland's national spirit and to stimulating the people's will to take up again the fight begun by the leaders and men and women who fought in Easter Week, 1916.

Thomas Ashe under British Army guard

Thomas Ashe

On 25 September 1917, Thomas Ashe died in Mountjoy Prison as a result of force-feeding. He had been on hunger strike for political status. When asked by the Lord Mayor of Dublin to end his protest, Ashe replied: "No. They have branded me a criminal. Even though I do die, I die in a good cause." Ashe was the first of 22 Irish republicans to die on hunger strike in the 20th century.

Verdict of the Jury in the Inquest of Thomas Ashe

We find that the deceased, Thomas Ashe... died of from heart failure and congestion of the lungs on the 25th September, 1917; that his death was caused by the punishment of taking away from the cell bed, bedding and boots, and allowing him to be on the cold floor for 50 hours, and then subjecting him to forcible feeding in his weak condition after hunger-striking for five or six days.

We censure the Castle Authorities for not acting more promptly, especially when the grave condition of the deceased and other prisoners was brought to their notice...

That the hunger strike was adopted against the inhuman punishment inflicted and a refusal to their demand to be treated as political prisoners...

Sinn Féin transformed

It was the Sinn Féin Ard Fheis of 25 October 1917 that committed the organisation for the first time to the establishment of an Irish Republic. The formula of words — devised by Eamon de Valera — in the new Constitution that stated "having achieved that status the Irish people may by referendum freely choose their own form of Government" was a concession to Arthur Griffith. He argued against the demand for a Republic, claiming that demands should be kept within achievable limits as he saw them. According to Thomas Dillon (Secretary of Sinn Féin in 1917), while Griffith did not argue within Sinn Féin for a monarchy, he did say to Dillon later that for the sake of stability he favoured a monarchy along Scandinavian lines. However, the Constitution adopted in the Mansion House on 25 October 1917 was clearly Republican and was widely understood as such. The first three clauses quoted here remain in the Sinn Féin Constitution to this day.

Sinn Féin Constitution, 1917

Whereas the people of Ireland never relinquished the claim to separate Nationhood, and

Whereas the Provisional Government of the Irish Republic, Easter 1916, in the name of the Irish people, and continuing the fight made by previous generations, reasserted the inalienable right of the Irish nation to Sovereign independence, and reaffirmed the determination of the Irish people to achieve it; and

Whereas the Proclamation of an Irish Republic, Easter 1916, and the supreme courage and glorious sacrifices of the men who gave their lives to maintain it, have united the people of Ireland under the flag of the Irish Republic, be it Resolved that we, the delegated representatives of the Irish People, in convention assembled, hereby declare the following to be the Constitution of Sinn Féin:-

1. The name of the organisation shall be Sinn Féin.

2. Sinn Féin aims at securing the international recognition of Ireland as an independent Irish Republic. Having achieved that status the Irish people may by referendum freely choose their own form of Government.

3. This object shall be attained through the Sinn Féin Organisation which shall, in the name of the sovereign Irish People -

(a) Deny the right and oppose the will of the British Parliament and British Crown or any other foreign government to legislate for Ireland;

(b) Make use of any and every means available to render impotent the power of England to hold Ireland in subjection by military force or otherwise.

National Unity against Conscription

By the spring of 1918, tens of thousands of Irishmen had died fighting in the British Army in the Great War. After 1916, recruiting had slowed as Republicanism gained strength and as the futility of the imperialist war became evident to more and more people. Nearly four years into the war there was no victory in sight for the British and they decided to impose conscription — compulsory military service — on Ireland. There was unprecedented unity in opposition. The anti-Conscription pledge was signed throughout Ireland on Sunday 21 April, 1918. On 23 April, there was a National General Strike called by the Irish Trades Union Congress which shut down almost the entire country.

Ireland and Conscription
Unanimous Declaration of the Mansion House Conference

Thursday, 18th April, 1918. Presided over by the Right Ho. The Lord Mayor of Dublin.

Present: Eamon de Valera, Arthur Griffith, John Dillon MP, Joseph Devlin MP, William O'Brien MP, T.M. Healy MP, W. O'Brien, President Irish Trades Union Congress. Thomas Johnson (Belfast), M. Egan J.P, T.C (Cork).

Taking our stand on Ireland's separate and distinct nationhood, and affirming the principle of liberty, that the government of nations derive their just powers from the consent of the governed, we deny the right of the British government or any external authority to impose compulsory military service in Ireland against the clearly expressed will of the Irish people.

The passing of the Conscription Bill by the British House of Commons must be regarded as a declaration of war on the Irish nation. The alternative to accepting it as such is to surrender our liberties and to acknowledge ourselves slaves. It is in direct violation of the rights of small nationalities to self-determination, which even the Prime Minister of England — now preparing to employ naked militarism and force his Act upon Ireland — himself officially announced as an essential condition for peace at the Peace Congress.

The attempt to enforce it will be an unwarrantable aggression, which we call upon all Irishmen to resist by the most effective means at their disposal.

Anti-Conscription pledge

Denying the right of the British Government to enforce compulsory service on this country, we pledge ourselves solemnly to one another to resist Conscription by the most effective means at our disposal.

Sinn Féin General Election Manifesto, 1918

The landslide for Sinn Féin in the General Election of 1918 swept away the Irish Parliamentary Party and placed the Irish demand for independence before the world. Sinn Féin fought the election on a Republican manifesto. It was censored by the British authorities. Passages underlined and in bold below are those cut by the British censor.

The coming General Election is fraught with vital possibilities for the future of our nation. Ireland is faced with the question of whether this generation wills it that she is to march out into the full sunlight of freedom, or is to remain in the shadow of **a base imperialism that has brought and ever will bring in its train naught but evil for our race.**

Sinn Féin gives Ireland the opportunity of vindicating her honour and pursuing with renewed confidence the path of national salvation by rallying to the flag of the Irish Republic.

Sinn Féin aims at securing the establishment of that Republic.

1. By withdrawing the Irish Representation from the British Parliament and by denying the right **and opposing the will** of the British Government **or any other foreign Government to legislate for Ireland.**

2. **By making use of any and every means available to render impotent the power of England to hold Ireland in subjection by military force or otherwise.**

3. By the establishment of a constituent assembly comprising persons chosen by Irish constituencies as the supreme national authority to speak and act in the name of the Irish people, and to develop Ireland's social, political and industrial life, for the welfare of the whole people of Ireland.

4. By appealing to the Peace Conference for the establishment of Ireland as an independent nation. At that conference the future of the nations of the world will be settled on the principle of government by consent of the governed. Ireland's claim to the application of that principle in her favour is not based on any accidental situation arising from the war. It is older than many if not all of the present belligerents....

Sinn Féin stands **less for a political party than** for the Nation; it represents the old tradition of nationhood **handed on from dead generations; it stands by the Proclamation of the Provisional Government of Easter 1916**, reasserting the inalienable right of Irish Nation to sovereign independence, reaffirming the determination of the Irish people to achieve it, and guaranteeing within the independent nation equal rights and equal opportunities to all its citizens...

The policy of our opponents stands condemned on any test, whether principle of expediency. **The right of a nation to sovereign independence rests upon immutable natural law and cannot be made the subject of a compromise.** Any attempt to barter away the sacred and inviolable rights of nationhood begins in dishonour and is bound to end in disaster. The enforced exodus of millions of our people, the decay of our industrial life, the ever-increasing financial plunder of our country, the whittling down of the demand for the 'Repeal of the Union' by the first Irish Leader to plead in the Hall of the Conqueror to that of Home Rule on the Statute Book, and finally the contemplated mutilation of our country by Partition, are some of the ghastly results of a policy that leads to national ruin.

Those who have harnessed the people of Ireland to England's war-chariot, ignoring the fact that only a freely-elected government in a free Ireland has power to decide the question of peace and war, have forfeited the right to speak for the Irish people...

Overwhelming Sinn Féin Victory

The landslide for Sinn Féin in the General Election of 1918 swept away the Irish Parliamentary Party and placed the Irish demand for independence before the world.

Seats in Ireland - 105

Sinn Féin - 73

Unionists - 26

Irish Parliamentary Party - 6

Ulster

Unionists - 22

Sinn Féin - 10

Irish Parliamentary Party - 5

Leinster

Sinn Féin - 26

Unionists - 1

Connacht

Sinn Féin - 13

Munster

Sinn Féin - 23

Irish Parliamentary Party - 1

Universities

Unionists - 3

Sinn Féin - 1

GENERAL ELECTION.

Manifesto to the Irish People.

THE coming General Election is fraught with vital possibilities for the future of our nation. Ireland is faced with the question whether this generation wills it that she is to march out into the full sunlight of freedom, or is to remain in the shadow of a base imperialism that has brought and ever will bring in its train naught but evil for our race.

Sinn Fein gives Ireland the opportunity of vindicating her honour and pursuing with renewed confidence the path of national salvation by rallying to the flag of the Irish Republic.

Sinn Fein aims at securing the establishment of that Republic.

1. By withdrawing the Irish Representation from the British Parliament and by denying the right and opposing the will of the British Government or any other foreign Government to legislate for Ireland.

2. By making use of any and every means available to render impotent the power of England to hold Ireland in subjection by military force or otherwise.

3. By the establishment of a constituent assembly comprising persons chosen by Irish constituencies as the supreme national authority to speak and act in the name of the Irish people, and to develop Ireland's social, political and industrial life, for the welfare of the whole people of Ireland.

4. By appealing to the Peace Conference for the establishment of Ireland as an Independent Nation. At that conference the future of the Nations of the world will be settled on the principle of government by consent of the governed. Ireland's claim to the application of that principle in her favour is not based on any accidental situation arising from the war. It is based on our unbroken tradition of nationhood, on a unity in a national name which has never been challenged, on our possession of a distinctive national culture and social order, on the moral courage and dignity of our people in the face of alien aggression, on the fact that in nearly every generation, and five times within the past 120 years our people have challenged in arms the right of England to rule this country. On these incontrovertible facts is based the claim that our people have beyond question established the right to be accorded all the powers of a free nation.

Sinn Fein stands less for a political party than for the Nation ; it represents the old tradition of nationhood handed on from dead generations; it stands by the Proclamation of the Provisional Government of Easter, 1916, reasserting the inalienable right of the Irish Nation to sovereign independence ; reaffirming the determination of the Irish people to achieve it, and guaranteeing within the independent Nation equal rights and equal opportunities to all its citizens.

Believing that the time has arrived when Ireland's voice for the principle of untrammelled National self-determination should be heard above every interest of party or class, Sinn Fein will oppose at the Polls every individual candidate who does not accept this principle.

The policy of our opponents stands condemned on any test, whether of principle or expediency. The right of a nation to sovereign independence rests upon immutable natural law and cannot be made the subject of a compromise. Any attempt to barter away the sacred and inviolate rights of nationhood begins in dishonour and is bound to end in disaster. The enforced exodus of millions of our people, the decay of our industrial life, the ever-increasing financial plunder of our country, the whittling down of the demand for the " Repeal of the Union," voiced by the first Irish Leader to plead in the Hall of the Conqueror to that of Home Rule on the Statute Book, and finally the contemplated mutilation of our country by partition, are some of the ghastly results of a policy that leads to national ruin.

Those who have endeavoured to harness the people of Ireland to England's war-chariot, ignoring the fact that only a freely-elected Government in a free Ireland has power to decide for Ireland the question of peace and war, have forfeited the right to speak for the Irish people. The Green Flag turned red in the hands of the Leaders, but that shame is not to be laid at the doors of the Irish people unless they continue a policy of sending their representatives to an alien and hostile assembly, whose powerful influence has been sufficient to destroy the integrity and sap the independence of their representatives. Ireland must repudiate the men who, in a supreme crisis for the nation, attempted to sell her birthright for the vague promises of English Ministers, and who showed their incompetence by failing to have even these promises fulfilled.

The present Irish members of the English Parliament constitute an obstacle to be removed from the path that leads to the Peace Conference. By declaring their will to accept the status of a province instead of boldly taking their stand upon the right of the nation, they supply England with the only subterfuge at her disposal for obscuring the issue in the eyes of the world. By their persistent endeavours to induce the young manhood of Ireland to don the uniform of our seven-century-old oppressor, and place their lives at the disposal of the military machine that holds our Nation in bondage, they endeavour to barter away and even to use against their own great asset still left to our Nation after the havoc of centuries.

Sinn Fein goes to the polls handicapped by all the arts and contrivances that a powerful and unscrupulous enemy can use against us. Conscious of the power of Sinn Fein to secure the freedom of Ireland the British Government would destroy it. Sinn Fein, however, goes to the polls confident that the people of this ancient nation will be true to the old cause and will vote for the men who stand by the principles of Tone, Emmet, Mitchell, Pearse and Connolly, the men who disdain to whine to the enemy for favours, the men who hold that Ireland must be as free as England or Holland, or Switzerland or France, and whose demand is that the only status befitting this ancient realm is the status of a free nation.

Issued by the Standing Committee of Sinn Fein.

Majority vote for Sinn Féin - 70 per cent

24 of the 32 Counties returned only Sinn Féin TDs.

Of the nine counties of Ulster, the Unionists polled a majority in four — Antrim, Armagh, Derry and Down.

Of Dublin's 11 TDs, all but one were Sinn Féin.

The only woman elected was Constance Markievicz, representing St. Patrick's Ward in Dublin's Liberties.

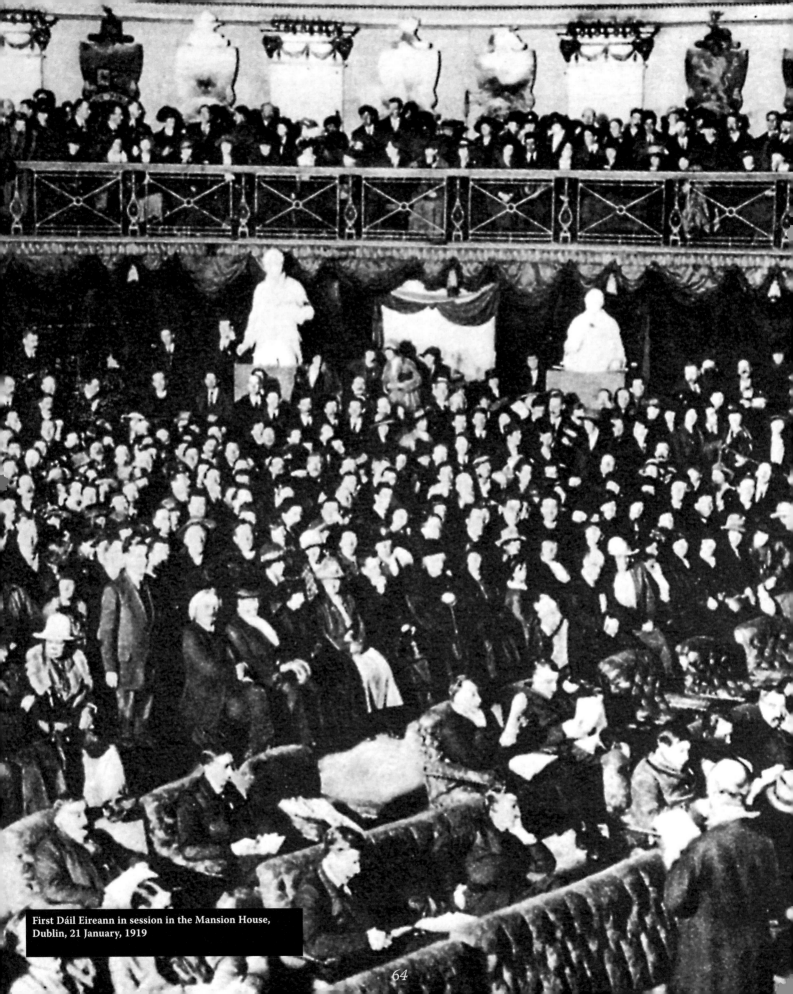

First Dáil Eireann in session in the Mansion House,
Dublin, 21 January, 1919

A nation at war
1919-1922

An Chéad Dáil Éireann

Ar an 8ú Eanáir 1919 d'eisigh George Plunkett TD cuireadh do gach Teachta tofa in Éirinn san olltoghchán freastal ar Dáil Éireann. Tionóladh an Chéad Dáil Éireann ar an 21ú Eanáir 1919 i dTeach an Ard Mhéara, Baile Átha Cliath. Bhí 30 Teachta Dála i láthair. Bhí 36 Teachtaí "faoi ghlas ag Gallaibh" mar a dúradh nuair a glaodh amach a n-ainmneacha, agus bhí daoine eile "ar díbirt ag Gallaibh" nó ar a gcoimeád.

Nóta ar an Ghaeilge: Seo thíos na cáipéisí ón gCéad Dáil mar a foilsíodh iad, le sean-litriú na Gaeilge mar a bhí sí in úsáid ag an am. 'Saorstát' (in ionad 'Poblacht') an aistiriú a bhí ann ar 'Republic'. 'Saorstát' an ainm a tugadh do stát na 26 Chontae nuair a bunaíodh é.

Faisnéis Neamhspleachais

De bhrigh gur dual do mhuinntir na hÉireann bheith n-a saor náisiún.

Agus de bhrigh nár staon muintir na hÉireann riamh le seacht gcéad bliadhain ó dhiúltadh d'annsmacht Gall agus ó chur ina choinnibh go minic le neart airm.

Agus de bhrígh ná fuil de bhunadhas agus ná raibh riamh de bhunadhas le dlighe Shasana san tír seo acht foiréigean agus calaois, agus ná fuil de thaca leis ach sealbh lucht airm i n-aimhdheóin dearbhthola muinntire na hÉireann.

Agus de bhrigh go ndeárna Saor-Arm na hÉireann Saorstát Éireann d'fhorfhógairt i mBaile Átha Cliath Seachtmhain na Cásca 1916 ar son muinntire na hÉireann.

Agus de bhrigh go bhfuil muinntir na hÉireann lán-cheaptha ar neamhspléadhchus iomlán do bhaint amach agus do chosaint dóibh fhéin d'fhonn leas an phobuil do chur chun cinn, an ceart d'athchur ar a bhonnaibh, an tsíothcháin in Éirinn agus caradas le náisiúnaibh eile do chur i n-áirithe dhóibh féin agus féineachus náisiúan tsíothcháin in Éirinn agus caradas le náisiúnaibh eile do chur i n-áirithe dhóibh féin agus féineachus náisiúnta do cheapadh go mbeidh toil na ndaoine mar bhunudhas leis agus cothrom cirt is caoitheamhlachta dá bhárr ag gach duine i nÉirinn.

Agus de bhrigh go ndeárna muinntir na hÉireann, agus sinn i mbéal ré nuadha de stair an domhain, feidhm a bhaint as an Olltoghadh, Mí na Nodlag, 1918, chun a dhearbhughadh de bhreis adhbhalmhóir gur toil leó bheith díleas do Shaorstát Éireann.

Ar an adhbhar son deinimídne .i. na teachtaí atá toghtha ag muinntir na hÉireann agus sinn i nDáil Chomhairle i dteannta a chéile, bunughadh Saorstáit d'áth-dheimhniughadh i n-ainm náisiún na hÉireann agus sinn féin do chur fá gheasaibh an deimhniughadh so do chur i bhfeidhm ar gach slighe ar ár gcumas.

Órduighmíd ná fuil de chomhacht ag éinne ach amháin ag na Teachtaíbh toghtha ag muinntir na hÉireann dlighthe dhéanamh gur dual do mhuinntir na hÉireann géilleadh dhóibh, agus ná fuil de pháirliment ann go mbeidh an náisiún umhal do ach amháin Dáil Éireann.

Dearbhuighmíd ná fuilingeóchaimíd go bráth an cumhangcas atá dá dhéanamh ag an annsmacht Ghallda ar ár gceart náisiúnta agus éilighmíd ar chamthaí na Sasanach imtheacht ar fad as ár dtír.

Ilighimíd ar gach saornáisiún ar domhan neamhspleádhchus na hÉireann d'admháil agus fógraimíd gurab éigean ár neamhspleádhchus chun síothcháin a chur i n-áirithe do'n domhan.

I n-ainm muinntire na hÉireann cuirimíd ár gcinneamhaint fé chomairce Dhia an Uile-Chomhacht do chuir misneach agus buan-tseasamhacht n-ár sinnsear chun leanamhaint leó go treun les na céadta bliadhain gcoinnibh tíoránachta gan truagh gan taise: agus de bhrigh gur móide an neart an ceart a bheith againn san troid d'fhágadar mar oighreacht againn, aithchuingimíd ar Dhia A bheannacht do bhronnadh orainn i gcóir an treasa deiridh den chomhrac go bfhuilmid fé gheasaibh leanmhaint do go dtí go mbainfeam amach an tsaoirse.

Declaration of Independence

Whereas the Irish people is by right a free people:

And Whereas for seven hundred years the Irish people has never ceased to repudiate and has repeatedly protested in arms against foreign usurpation:

And Whereas English rule in this country is, and always has been, based upon force and fraud and maintained by military occupation against the declared will of the people:

And Whereas the Irish Republic was proclaimed in Dublin on Easter Monday, 1916, by the Irish Republican Army acting on behalf of the Irish people:

And Whereas the Irish people is resolved to secure and maintain its complete independence in order to promote the common weal, to re-establish justice, to provide for future defence, to ensure peace at home and goodwill with all nations and to constitute a national polity based upon the people's will with equal right and equal opportunity for every citizen:

And Whereas at the threshold of a new era in history the Irish electorate has in the General Election of December, 1918, seized the first occasion to declare by an overwhelming majority its firm allegiance to the Irish Republic:

Now, therefore, we, the elected Representatives of the ancient Irish people in National Parliament assembled, do, in the name of the Irish nation, ratify the establishment of the Irish Republic and pledge ourselves and our people to make this declaration effective by every means at our command:

We ordain that the elected Representatives of the Irish people alone have power to make laws binding on the people of Ireland, and that the Irish Parliament is the only Parliament to which that people will give its allegiance:

We solemnly declare foreign government in Ireland to be an invasion of our national right which we will never tolerate, and we demand the evacuation of our country by the English Garrison

Constance Markievicz, Minister for Labour, First Dáil

We claim for our national independence the recognition and support of every free nation in the world, and we proclaim that independence to be a condition precedent to international peace hereafter:

In the name of the Irish people we humbly commit our destiny to Almighty God who gave our fathers the courage and determination to persevere through long centuries of a ruthless tyranny, and strong in the justice of the cause which they have handed down to us, we ask His divine blessing on this the last stage of the struggle we have pledged ourselves to carry through to Freedom.

Clár Oibre Poblachtánach

Dearbhuighimíd, i mbriathraibh for-fhógra Saorstáit Éireann go bhfuil sé de cheart ag muinntir na hÉireann sealbh na hÉireann do bheith aca agus cinneamhain an náisiúin do bheith fé n-a riar, agus nách féidir an ceart san do bhaint díobh; agus fébh mar dubhairt ár gceud Uachtarán Pádraig Mac Phiarais, dearbhuighimíd gur ceart go mbeadh, ní amháin fir agus mná na hÉireann, acht adhbhar maoine na hÉireann fé riaradh an náisiúin, idir talamh agus gustal na hÉireann, gach sadhas maoine agus gach gléas chun maoin do sholáthairt dá bhfuil san tír; agus athfhógraimíd an rud d'fhógair an Piarsach gur dual go mbéadh tosach ag ceart an phobuil chun leasa an phobuil ar cheart an duine chun seilbhe fé leith.

Dearbhuighmíd gur mian linn an ceart, an tsaoirse agus cothrom do chách a bheith mar bhuntacaí riaghlughadh na tíre, agus ná fuil d'urradhas le buanughadh Riaghaltais ná saorthoiliughadh na ndaoine chuige ach é.

Dearbhuighimíd go bhfuil sé de dhualgas ar gach fear agus gach mnaoi bheith umhal, díleas, freagarthach agus freastalach don Phobalacht; agus go bhfuil sé de dhualgas ar an náisiún feuchaint chuige go mbeidh caoi ag gach duine san tír ar a cheart agus a acfuinn féin do chur i bhfeidhm ar mhaithe le leas an phobuil. Mar chúiteamh ar fhreagra is freastal na ndaoine, dearbhuighimíd i n-ainm an tSaorstáit, gur dual do gach duine a cion féin de thoradh saothair an náisiúin a bheith aige.

Is é an príomhchúram a bheidh ar Riaghaltas an tSaorstáit ná gleusa soláthar chun leas corpordha, leas spioradálta agus leas inntleachta na leanbhaí do chur i n-áirithe dhóibh; feuchaint chuige ná béidh an t-ocras ná an fuacht ag goilleamhaint ar éin leanbh de cheal bídh, eudaigh ná dín tighe; acht go bhfaghaidh siad gach cóir agus gleus is gádh dhóibh chun teagaisc agus taithighe ceart do thabhairt dóibh i gcóir na hoibre a bheidh le deunamh aca mar chomhaltaí den tSaorstát Gaedhealach.

**Women protest against the execution of
Republican prisoners by the British
Government, 1920**

Is follus do Shaorstát Éireann nach foláir an dlighe gránna iasachta a bhainnean le Tighthe na mBocht i nÉirinn agus gach a ngabhann leis de chéimsíos is de náire, do chur ar ceal, agus plean éifeachtach éigin do cheapadh a bheidh oireamhnach don tír chun aire cheart do thabhairt do sheandaoinibh agus do lagaibh an náisiúin, daoine a thuilleann freastal agus buidheachas ón náisiún I n-ionad tarcuisne agus neamhshuime. Na theannta son, beidh sé de chúram ar an Saorstát gach gleus is áis dár ghádh a chur i bhfeidhm chun sláinte an phobuil agus leas corpordha an náisiúin, agus leas anama an náisiúin dá bhárr do chur i n-áirithe dhóibh.

Beidh sé de dhualgas orainn cabhrughadh le meudughadh gustail an náisiúin, an talamh a dheunamh níos torthamhla agus níos iontsaothruighthe; mianach na hÉireann, a portaigh mhóna, a cuid iascaigh, a bealaigh uisce, agus a cuanta do chur chun críche i ceart chun tairbhe muinntire na hÉireann.

Beidh sé de dhualgas ar an Saorstát gach níd is gádh do dheunamh chun ár ndéantúsa d'aithbheóchaint is do neartughadh agus feuchaint chuige go saothróchfar iad do réir "comhar oibre" ar an gcuma is feárr 's is oireamhnaighe 's is mó raghaidh i dtairbhe do chách. Cuirfar feadhmannaigh ó Éirinn go tíortha thar lear d'fhonn ceannuidheacht agus tráchtáil do chur chun cinn idir Éire agus na tíortha úd, a raghaidh i leas don tír seo agus dosna tíortha eile. Nuair a thabharfaidh an Saorstát fé thráchtáil an náisiúin, idir díoluidheacht agus ceannuidheacht, do riarad, beidh sé de dhualgas ar an Saorstát gan biadh ná earraí eile go bhfuil gádh leó do leigint thar lear ó Éirinn go mbeidh a leórdhóthain fachta ag muinntir na hÉireann, agus a sáith i dtaisce aca i gcóir an ama le teacht.

Beidh sé de chúram ar Riaghaltas an Náisiúin, leis, a iarraidh ar Riaghaltaisí tíortha eile cabhrughadh agus comhoibriughadh ar chomh-chéim leó chun dlighthe i dtaobh gnáthshaoghail agus gnáth-oibre an phobuil do cheapadh a chuirfidh feabhas mór ar an gcórughadh saoghail is saothair a bhíonn le fághail ag lucht oibre.

Democratic Programme

We declare in the words of the Irish Republican Proclamation the right of the people of Ireland to the ownership of Ireland, and to the unfettered control of Irish destinies to be indefeasible, and in the language of our first President, Pádraíg Mac Phiarais, we declare that the Nation's sovereignty extends not only to all men and women of the Nation, but to all its material possessions, the Nation's soil and all its resources, all the wealth and all the wealth-producing processes within the Nation, and with him we reaffirm that all right to private property must be subordinated to the public right and welfare.

We declare that we desire our country to be ruled in accordance with the principles of Liberty,

Equality, and Justice for all, which alone can secure permanence of Government in the willing adhesion of the people.

We affirm the duty of every man and woman to give allegiance and service to the Commonwealth, and declare it is the duty of the Nation to assure that every citizen shall have opportunity to spend his or her strength and faculties in the service of the people. In return for willing service, we, in the name of the Republic, declare the right of every citizen to an adequate share of the produce of the Nation's labour.

It shall be the first duty of the Government of the Republic to make provision for the physical, mental and spiritual well-being of the children, to secure that no child shall suffer hunger or cold from lack of food, clothing, or shelter, but that all shall be provided with the means and facilities requisite for their proper education and training as Citizens of a Free and Gaelic Ireland.

The Irish Republic fully realises the necessity of abolishing the present odious, degrading and foreign Poor Law System, substituting therefore a sympathetic native scheme for the care of the Nation's aged and infirm, who shall not be regarded as a burden, but rather entitled to the Nation's gratitude and consideration. Likewise it shall be the duty of the Republic to take such measures as will safeguard the health of the people and ensure the physical as well as the moral well-being of the Nation.

It shall be our duty to promote the development of the Nation's resources, to increase the productivity of its soil, to exploit its mineral deposits, peat bogs, and fisheries, its waterways and harbours, in the interests and for the benefit of the Irish people.

It shall be the duty of the Republic to adopt all measures necessary for the recreation and invigoration of our Industries, and to ensure their being developed on the most beneficial and progressive co-operative and industrial lines. With the adoption of an extensive Irish Consular Service, trade with foreign Nations shall be revived on terms of mutual advantage and goodwill, and while undertaking the organisation of the Nation's trade, import and export, it shall be the duty of the Republic to prevent the shipment from Ireland of food and other necessaries until the wants of the Irish people are fully satisfied and the future provided for.

It shall also devolve upon the National Government to seek co-operation of the Governments of other countries in determining a standard of Social and Industrial Legislation with a view to a general and lasting improvement in the conditions under which the working classes live and labour.

The Black and Tans

73

Soloheadbeg

It was a coincidence, but a very important one, that the first significant armed confrontation between the newly reorganised Irish Volunteers — quickly to become more generally known as the Irish Republican Army — and the British Crown Forces occurred on the same day that the First Dáil Éireann met. At Soloheadbeg, County Tipperary, Seán Treacy, Dan Breen and six other Volunteers remained for five days in ambush positions awaiting the arrival of a consignment of gelignite for the local quarry. When it arrived on 21 January the armed guard of two RIC men refused to surrender and they were shot dead. Here Dan Breen describes the hostile reaction the IRA column met from many in the wake of the ambush.

We were still within a radius of ten miles from Soloheadbeg. Police and military were scouring the countryside for us, searching houses, ditches and woods. The clergy, the public and the press had unanimously condemned our action. Our only consoling thought was that the men of '98, the Fenians of '67 and the men of 1916 were condemned in their day. As the cause of these men had been vindicated, so too would our cause when the scales fell from the eyes of the people. At the time, however, scarce a word would be heard in our defence. Our point of view was not even listened to. The people had voted for a Republic; now they seemed to have abandoned us who tried to bring that Republic nearer, for we had taken them at their word.

Our former friends shunned us. They preferred the drawing room as a battleground; the political resolution rather than the gun as their offensive weapon. We had heard the gospel of freedom preached; we believed in it, we wanted to be free, and we were prepared to give our lives as proof of the faith that was in us. But those who preached the gospel were not prepared to practise it.

Oath of allegiance to the Irish Republic

On 20 August 1919, Dáil Éireann agreed that all TDs and IRA Volunteers should take the following oath:

I, A.B., do solemnly swear (or affirm) that I do not and shall not yield a voluntary support to any pretended Government, authority or power within Ireland hostile and inimical thereto, and I do further swear (or affirm) that to the best of my knowledge and ability I will support and defend the Irish Republic and the Government of the Irish Republic, which is Dáil Éireann, against all enemies, foreign and domestic, and I will bear true faith and allegiance to the same, and that I take this obligation freely without any mental reservation or purpose of evasion, so help me, God

Dáil Éireann banned — Partition Bill introduced

On 10 September 1919, the British Government banned Dáil Éireann. On 22 December, the British Prime Minister, Lloyd George, introduced the Government of Ireland Bill in the House of Commons. To Republicans it was the Partition Bill. Lloyd George threatened further coercion. His answer came in the Municipal Elections in January 1920 when 72 out of 127 towns and cities in Ireland elected Sinn Féin majorities. The spirit of the time is summed up in this piece by Erskine Childers in the Irish Bulletin, *the underground newspaper of Dáil Éireann:*

You own a third of the earth by conquest; you have great armies, a navy so powerful that it can starve a whole continent, and a superabundance of every instrument of destruction that science can devise. You wield the greatest aggregate of material force ever concentrated in the hands of one power; and while canting about your championship of small nations, you use it to crush liberty in ours. We are a small people with a population dwindling without cessation under your rule. We have no armaments nor any prospect of obtaining them. Nevertheless we accept your challenge and we will fight you...

Tomás MacCurtáin

On 20 March 1920, the Sinn Féin Lord Mayor of Cork City, Tomás MacCurtáin, was murdered in his home by members of the Royal Irish Constabulary. He had been elected Mayor the previous January. He was succeeded as Mayor by Traolach MacSuibhne (Terence MacSwiney).

Unanimous inquest verdict

Tomás MacCurtáin

We find that the late Alderman MacCurtáin, Lord Mayor of Cork, died from shock and haemorrhage caused by bullet wounds, and that he was wilfully murdered under circumstances of the most callous brutality, and that the murder was organised and carried out by the Royal Irish Constabulary, officially directed by the British Government, and we return a verdict of wilful murder against David Lloyd George, Prime Minister of England; Lord French, Lord Lieutenant of Ireland; Ian McPherson, late Chief Secretary of Ireland; Acting Inspector General Smith of the Royal Irish Constabulary; Divisional Inspector Clayton of the Royal Irish Constabulary; District Inspector Swanzy and some unknown members of the Royal Irish Constabulary. We strongly condemn the system at present in vogue of carrying out raids at unreasonable hours. We tender to Mrs. MacCurtáin and family our sincerest sympathy. We extend to the citizens of Cork our sympathy in the loss they have sustained by the death of one so eminently capable of directing their civic administration.

The funeral of Traolach MacSuibhne attended by thousands in Cork City.

Traolach MacSuibhne writes to the British Home Secretary

Traolach MacSuibhne succeeded Tomás MacCurtáin as Lord Mayor of Cork. When he was arrested in the City Hall in August 1920, he embarked on a hunger strike. He was taken to Brixton Prison in London. On 20 September, he wrote the following letter to the British Home Secretary Edward Shortt. MacSuibhne died on 25 October, the 74th day of his hunger strike.

The Medical Commissioner of Prisons... impressed on me that my health was in a very dangerous condition. He impressed on me the gravity of my state and then read a document from you, warning me that I would not be released and the consequences of my refusing to take food would rest with myself.

Nevertheless, the consequences will rest with you. My undertaking on the day of my alleged court martial that I would be free alive or dead within a month will be fulfilled. It appears from your communication that my release is to be in death. In that event, the British Government can boast of having killed two Lord Mayors of the same City, within six months — an achievement without parallel in the history of oppression. Knowing the revolution of opinion that will thereby be caused throughout the civilised world and the consequent accession to Ireland in her hour of trial, I am reconciled to a premature grave.

Tom Barry at an IRA training camp

Popular support for the IRA

The Flying Columns of the IRA could not have operated in 1920 and '21 without popular support in the countryside. In his book, 'Guerilla Days in Ireland', Tom Barry describes one example of that support.

On a February day four of us left the Flying Column to visit the parents of Lieutenant Patrick Crowley who had been killed by the Essex Regiment. We came out from a wood at the back of the place where their home once stood, about five hundred yards from Kilbrittain Black and Tan Post. Unseen we approached the destroyed house and saw Mrs. Crowley sitting on a stool in the yard, gazing thoughtfully at the ruins of the blown up and burned out house, while Mr. Crowley moved some rubble to strengthen the little henhouse which alone had escaped the orgy of British destruction. Those two, near the close of their days, he, grey-bearded, thin and hardy, she ageing and frail looking, neatly dressed in black, were alone. Paddy had been killed by the British a week previously, Denis lay badly hurt in a British jail after a merciless beating by his captors. Con, one of our best fighters, was also a prisoner under the name of Patrick Murphy, and the shadow of death hung over him too, for should he be recognised, another Crowley would die for Ireland. The fourth and remaining son, Mick, seriously wounded early in the struggle, was a leading Flying Column Officer, and his chance of survival did not appear to be high as he, too, was a most active and daring officer. The two daughters, Ciss and Bridie, among the most excellent of our Cumann na mBan, were absent on IRA work and would not return until late that night. The sorrow and sufferings of this ageing couple must have weighed heavily upon them, but there were no signs of weakness or complaints as they listened to our words of sympathy at the death of their fine son. They were indomitable, unbreakable and proud of the part all their children were playing in the battle for freedom. To them, Pat had died well for Ireland, and it was unthinkable that any of their other sons would not fight equally well until the end. It was God's will that Pat had died, and perhaps he would see that the others would be spared. And one day when the British were driven out they would rebuild their home.

Who can fully estimate the value of men and women like those in a Nation's fight against alien rule? Their spirit and their faith in the justice of their cause did not allow of defeat at the hands of Imperialist mercenaries. British guns were not able to cow them, British money could not buy them, nor could British guile and duplicity wean them from their support of the Irish Republican Army, for indeed, they were as truly soldiers of the Resistance Movement as any Volunteer of the Flying Column.

A scene during the Truce

Arthur Griffith, Eamon de Valera, Laurence O'Neill and Michael Collins at Croke Park, 1921

Sydney Gifford Czira describes a scene outside Dublin's Mansion House during the Truce. It reflects the initial atmosphere of optimism when the Truce between the Republican forces and the British was declared in July 1921.

Griffith appeared, walking very erect, with his face as immobile as a marble image. Then with a war whoop 'Vive Sinn Féin' a Frenchwoman flung her arms round Griffith's neck, and kissed him warmly on both cheeks. Griffith's reaction to this embarrassing experience can readily be imagined. The thoughts that were passing through the minds of some of the crowd were well summed up by two young Dublin girls, who were watching the incident. 'God help the poor man,' said one of them sympathetically, as soon as she was able to draw her breath. 'Has that one no shame?' 'Oh Janey Mac,' replied the other, 'I'd as soon kiss the Rock of Cashel.'

Mary MacSwiney speaks against the Treaty

Cumann na mBan and the women of Sinn Féin were almost unanimously opposed to the Treaty signed in London on 6 December 1921. Mary MacSwiney TD spoke for them in the Dáil's Treaty debate. Her speech throws an interesting light on views of Sinn Féin before and after 1917:

In trying to make some amusing points — some flippant points against one of the Members of this assembly — the last speaker mentioned Sinn Féin, that they were members of Sinn Féin once together, and all Sinn Féin stood for then was the King, Lords, and Commons of Ireland. That is perfectly true of many Members here. I for one say it has never been true of me, or anyone belonging to me. We absolutely refused to join Sinn Féin until Sinn Féin became Republican. It is absolutely true to say that that Treaty as it is given to you was the be-all and the end-all of Sinn Féin's existence up to 1918. It is the darling and the pet of Mr. Arthur Griffith's life. He has talked to us; he has shown how the Irish Party were fooled by Lloyd George or Lloyd George's predecessors. He has talked about 1782 and getting back to it. Some of us in 1917 had some trouble to make him use the word "Republic". He did not believe in a Republic. He is the one man of the five delegates who has shown that he does not believe in a Republic. Now that is to him an honest document. Sinn Féin up to 1918 was not Republican,

Mary MacSwiney

and in 1917 some of us were wondering very strongly whether we ought or ought not adopt another organisation altogether which would be definitely Republican, but we preferred to make that one that was in existence, and all the common members of which became definitely Republican after 1916 the organisation, if the founder and advocate of it would stand for complete independence. We wanted to get done with 1782ism, and we will not go back to it. And it is absolutely true to say that many men here who are now honest Republicans, in spite of the sneers, joined Sinn Féin and were good members of Sinn Féin, while half-measures were possible. Half-measures are no longer possible, because on the 21st of January, 1919, this assembly, elected by the will of the sovereign people of Ireland, declared by the will of the people the Republican form of Government as the best for Ireland, and cast off for ever their allegiance to any foreigner. The people of Ireland will stand by that and refuse to take it up again...

This fight of ours has been essentially a spiritual fight; it has been a fight of right against wrong, a fight of a small people struggling for a spiritual ideal against a mighty rapacious and material Empire, and, as the things of the spirit have always prevailed, they prevail now. Up to last December we had won the admiration of the world for our honour, and I tell the world that the honour of Ireland is still unsullied, and that Ireland will show it, and will show that Ireland means fidelity to the Republic and not the driving of a coach-and-four through the oath which she will never consent to allow her Ministers to take. This is a spiritual fight of ours, but though we are idealists standing for a spiritual principle, we are practical idealists, and it is your idealist that is the real practical man, not your opportunist; and watch the opportunists in every generation and you will see nothing but broken hopes behind them. It is those who stand for the spiritual and the ideal that stand true and unflinching, and it is those who will win — not those who can inflict most but those who can endure most will conquer...

I speak for the living Republic, the Republic that cannot die. That document will never kill it, never. The Irish Republic was proclaimed and established by the men of Easter Week, 1916. The Irish Republican Government was established in January, 1919, and it has functioned since under such conditions that no country ever worked under before. That Republican Government is not now going to be fooled and destroyed by the Wizard of Wales. We beat him before and we shall beat him again, and I pray with all my heart and soul that a majority of the Members of this assembly will throw out that Treaty and that the minority will stand shoulder to shoulder with us in the fight to regain the position we held on the 4th of this month. I pray that once more; I pray that we will stand together, and the country will stand behind us. I have no doubt of that. I know the women of Ireland, and I know what they will say to the men that want to surrender, and therefore I beg of you to take the decision to throw out that Treaty. Register your votes against it, and do not commit the one unforgivable crime that has ever been committed by the representatives of the people of Ireland

The execution of Republican
prisoners by the British provoked
widespread public anger

Sinn Féin strives for unity

*The leaders of Sinn Féin were deeply divided on the Treaty. But efforts to find an
accommodation continued throughout the spring of 1922. They seemed to have succeeded on
23 May when the Sinn Féin Ard Fheis ratified a Pact agreed between Eamon De Valera and
Michael Collins. This centred on the forthcoming General Election for which a panel of
candidates was agreed. As the election was to be held in the 26 Counties only, clause (5) of
the Pact would allow sitting TDs for the Six-County area to continue as TDs in the Third
Dáil. The British Government vehemently opposed the Pact and it was broken by Michael
Collins on the eve of the poll. The new Free State constitution was withheld until polling day
itself, giving most voters no opportunity to read it. Pro-Treaty candidates won 58 seats to 36
for the Republicans.*

The Collins-De Valera Pact

We are agreed:

(1) That a National Coalition panel for this Third Dáil, representing both parties in the Dáil and
in the Sinn Féin Organisation, be sent forward, on the ground that the national position
requires the entrusting of the Government of the country into the joint hands of those who have
been the strength of the national situation during the last few years, without prejudice to their
present respective position.

(2) That this Coalition panel be sent forward as from the Sinn Féin organisation, the number
for each party being their present strength in the Dáil.

(3) That the candidates be nominated through each of the existing party Executives.

(4) That every and any interest is free to go up and contest the election equally with the National
Sinn Féin panel.

(5) That constituencies where an election is not held shall continue to be represented by their
present Deputies.

(6) That after the election the Executive shall consist of the President, elected as formerly; the
Minister for Defence, representing the Army; and nine other Ministers — five from the majority
party and four from the minority, each party to choose its own nominees. The allocation will
be in the hands of the President.

(7) That in the event of the Coalition government finding it necessary to dissolve, a General
Election will be held as soon as possible on adult suffrage.

Victims of the Belfast pogroms

As the partitioned Six Counties were transformed into the Orange state of 'Northern Ireland' in 1922, thousands of nationalists were forced from their jobs and homes. Sydney Gifford Czira, who wrote under the pen-name John Brennan, describes in Poblacht na hÉireann *the refugees from Belfast as they arrived in Dublin:*

The refugees are for the most part women and children. Their faces wear a haunted look, and some young mothers carrying little children in their arms have aged so much owing to their terrible trials that one can hardly believe they are still in their early 20s.

The refugees are met in Amiens Street station by volunteers in motor cars and driven to Marlboro Hall, where they are taken charge of by a matron and comfortably housed...

One of the women brought home to me forcibly the hopelessness of the positions of the Catholics by explaining that just as the Jews in Russia were compelled to live in one limited area called the ghetto, which was invaded and sacked by their enemies whenever race hatred was excited, so the Catholics in Belfast have to live within a prescribed district, entirely surrounded by a hostile population, and absolutely at their mercy when trouble starts.

Three nice little girls, sitting on the grass making a daisy chain, explained to me that they came from Weaver Street where the bomb was thrown amongst a crowd of children on the 13th February. Two of these children had been wounded by that bomb. They were little apprentices and had just come home from work. They were skipping on the road outside their own doors when without warning or any provocation a bomb was thrown amongst them, killing six and wounding 24 of their playmates. A few weeks later, on May 20th, the three streets comprising this area were swept with bullets, and the Specials came along and ordered all Catholics in the district – in all 116 householders and their families to leave the district. They were taken away in lorries by the military and brought to North Queen Street Schools, which are Catholic schools, and there left to find housing and safety as best they might....

A young mother, Mrs. McGowan, sitting with her two babies on the grass told me that every sudden noise made the children scream with terror since the frightful experience they had on 20th May. Some of the boys were playing cards outside their doors, everything was quiet and peaceful. Without any warning an Orange mob gathered at the street corner and began firing shots. Immediately the Specials came on the street, and for three quarters of an hour they rained bombs and bullets into the street. The British soldiers arrived on the scene and were supposed to give protection to the Catholics, but they did nothing to stop the Orangemen from looting.

The IRA-occupied Four Courts in flames after bombardment
by the Free State Army, June 1922

On the eve of Civil War

The opening salvo of the Civil War was fired on 28 June by the Free State Army with guns borrowed from the British garrison. Under pressure from the British Government, the Free State Government ordered the bombardment of the Four Courts which were occupied by the Irish Republican Army. The journalist R.M. Fox describes the scene at the Four Courts before the fighting began. He meets with Erskine Childers who was one of the first Republican prisoners executed by the Free State in November 1922.

While the discussions about the treaty dragged on, Rory O'Connor and his Republican followers suddenly seized the Four Courts — the principal law courts of Dublin. I passed the building the afternoon of the occupation, and saw the crowds gathered round the gates — old women in shawls, workless men and swarms of children, peering through the railings. Young volunteers were busy unwinding huge coils of barbed wire and fortifying the building. They looked to me like children playing at soldiers as they ran about dragging the wire after them in the yard. Big law books were piled in heaps to barricade the lower window. One pile, behind a broken pane, leaned outward in a tottering curve. Huge tomes filled with legal precedents surely had no precedent for this!

Later in the afternoon when I repassed the Four Courts three young volunteers had scrambled up to the top of the huge dome. Two sat on the edge with their legs dangling while the third, standing erect, was silhouetted against the sky, blowing stirring calls on his bugle. City men were just leaving their offices, and they scurried by, casting up glances of disgust. They represented the sober, conservative forces, the bugler stood for turmoil and unrest. There he was, unmoved by their hate, the spirit of youth blowing his fleeting blast of defiance to the world.

I went to see Erskine Childers, then editor of *The Republic of Ireland* — a weekly journal — and one of the strongest individual forces on the Republican side.

He was a slight, pale-faced man, with shy manner. I found it difficult to connect this reserved soft-spoken man with the stories I had heard of him as a revolutionary swashbuckler.

"I took the oath of allegiance to the Republic," he said, in his grave way. "I meant it then, I am keeping it now. Whether others meant it or not is for them to say.

"England has won a moral victory by the treaty. For the first time Ireland has been induced to abandon her claim to complete independence. Ireland can only remain united on the basis of this demand for independence, anything short of this is bound to create internal strife.

"It is the old story, some have wavered and given up the struggle. The rest of us are going on."

He seemed very much alone as he came down to show me out of the house.

"Make it clear that I am Irish, if you are writing about me," he said in parting. "I had an Irish mother, I spent my childhood in Ireland and I have chosen Irish citizenship."

Liam Mellows on Irish Freedom

Liam Mellows speaking at Bodenstown, June 1922.

Within days the Free State attacked the Four Courts, which Mellows and his comrades had occupied.

On 23 December 1922, the newspaper Voice of Labour *published the following article by Liam Mellows. It was a posthumous publication. Mellows had been executed in Mountjoy Prison on 8 December, together with Rory O'Connor, Joe McKelvey and Dick Barrett.*

When one talks of freedom for Ireland, one should have clearly in mind what is meant by Irish freedom. Freedom and independence, as used at present, are terms so ambiguous as to mean anything or nothing. The mere act of setting up a Republic is not a panacea for all the ills that trouble Ireland. Measures more far-reaching than that are required if Ireland is to enjoy real freedom.

The revolution going on in Ireland has a three-fold aspect, it is intellectual, it is political, it is economic. Of the intellectual aspect it is sufficient here to say that Ireland to be free, must be Irish, must be free from the domination of alien thought as from alien armies of occupation. The end of the political struggle, the withdrawal of the British army and British officials from Ireland, and the international recognition of the Irish Republic, will be the means of solving many of the present economic and social problems there, enabling the Government of Ireland to devote its entire attention to the internal matters of the country. Industries will receive encouragement; employment will increase; the natural resources of the country tapped; emigration stopped; education put on a proper basis, and direct contact with the outside world established.

Yet all this, resulting as it would in the country being richer and more prosperous, would not mean that the freedom of Ireland has been attained if the economic system remained unchanged. A political revolution in Ireland, without a coincident economic revolution, simply means a change of masters.

Instead of British capitalists waxing rich on the political and economic enslavement of Ireland, as at present, we would have Irish capitalists waxing rich on the political freedom, but continued enslavement of Ireland.

Ireland does not want a change of masters. It would be foolish, surely, to free Ireland from foreign tyranny today, and less than 20 years hence to have to free it from domestic tyranny. Therefore, the Irish Republic must have for its foundation the people. It is they who must own Ireland. It is they who are freeing Ireland; and it is for the people — all the people — that it is being done, not for any section or group.

Dáil Éireann had this clearly in mind when, at its first session, in January 1919, it issued its 'Programme of Democratic Policy'. In this programme it laid down that the soil of Ireland and all that grew upon it and lay under it, as well as all the wealth and wealth-producing processes in the country, should belong to the people.

In the last analysis, the fight between the Irish people and the British government is not alone between two nations; it is more than that; it is a struggle between two systems of civilisation, between the feudal system of England under its present guise of industrialism and the democratic system upon which the old civilisation of Ireland was built. A vestige of that civilisation remains in Ireland today. It is growing, expanding, and the end of foreign rule in Ireland will usher in not alone a new political era in Ireland, but a new economic one as well.

IRA unit in Grafton Street, Dublin, during the Civil War

Frank Ryan speaks at a mass
meeting to welcome
Republican prisoners released
in 1932

Carnival of Reaction
1923-1948

Brutality against women prisoners

Margaret Buckley

Margaret Buckley was a member of Inghinidhe na hÉireann, Cumann na mBan and Sinn Féin. Jailed after the 1916 Rising she later became a judge in the Dáil courts in Dublin, and a senior member of Sinn Féin. She was President of Sinn Féin from 1937 to 1950 and honorary vice-president from then until her death in 1962. In her book, 'The Jangle of Keys,' she describes her jail experience, including this from Mountjoy during the mass hunger strike of 1923:

Up the stairs they came, and by their voices we knew that at least some of them were under the influence of drink. We peeped out and saw that with the soldiers were five or six CID men, some of whom we knew well. They were making a lot of noise, and the Deputy, who accompanied them, seemed quite incapable of controlling them.

Suddenly we heard a key turn in our door; we were locked in. We started to dance 'The Walls of Limerick', singing for music, so that the noise outside was almost drowned by the noise inside. Paudeen [O'Keefe — the governor] was shouting at the top of his voice, but apparently had difficulty in getting himself heard.

After a while we heard the voices of some of the deportees as they passed our door, and we knew that they had been searched and were being passed out. The place was full of soldiers and they were sending in two at a time for search.

Presently a girl's shriek pierced the night and we nearly lost our reason. We battered at the locked door and shouted, but they jeered back at us, and even that was a relief, for we knew they would be too cowardly to jeer if anybody had been seriously hurt.

Then the little peephole shutter was pushed back and the mocking faces of our CID friends appeared; they talked in at us, passing insulting remarks. It is amazing how base even Irish mercenaries can become. We were powerless; our greatest weapon of defence was silence, and this angered them more. Meanwhile, Marie Deegan was collecting all the slops she could find in the room into one large vessel. Then creeping along the floor she suddenly raised herself and dashed its contents into the grinning, malicious faces gathered round the 'window'. Thereupon we broke silence and cheered, and it was just as well, for the spluttering language of the now dripping, begrimed ruffians was not nice to hear. It was a pandemonium; but they retreated from the window, and when at last our door was opened to permit us to pass between cordons of renegade Irishmen to the surgery, where the search was taking place, the CID was not in evidence.

It was nearly morning when it came to our turn. Each search had been accompanied by a row. This, of course, made for delay, and the resistance put up had disorganised all their plans. We trooped out, all together, when the door was opened, and were horrified by what met our eyes: girls with their clothes half torn off them, their faces and hands scratched, were being pushed down the stairs as they emerged from the surgery, and were laughed at and insulted by drunken soldiers.

As Judy Gaughan entered the room she was greeted by one of the searchers with 'Come on, Beauty.' Her response was more militant, and did not improve the facial contour or temper of her tormentor, who evidently did not expect what she got for her impudence. Maire Deegan was propelled out to the landing, showing a black eye, the outward and visible sign of her encounter within.

Josie Eivers and I were pushed forward into the surgery. There were three young women in the room; one, obviously, the worse for drink, sprawled on a chair; another, with an eye rapidly puffing up and changing colour, leaned against the mantle-piece; the third stood ready to paw me all over.

I had seen Judy flung down the stairs by a CID man, saved only from a fall, which would have maimed her for life, by clutching frantically at the balusters. I had seen Maire Comerford sit on a bench, like a stoic of old with tightly compressed lips, never emitting even a murmur, while a doctor (whom Paudeen had fetched) cut away her hair, and put three stitches in her head. I had seen Sighle Humphreys being dragged out, half conscious from the blow dealt her when she resisted the search.

I was looking now at a pool of blood at my feet, and I saw red. All the teachings of the good nuns who had charge of my youth, all the training and example of my home were for nought. My cave ancestors were in the ascendancy, and, towering over the creature who now approached to search me, I said, 'If you touch me, I'll choke the life out of you.' At that moment I felt quite capable of doing it, and I must have looked it, for the poor thing simply said: 'Go on,' and Josie and I 'went on' out to the waiting lorry.

I have always felt a little ashamed of my primitive impulse that night; my conduct, to say the least of it, was unladylike.

At last all were out, the soldiers took their places in the lorries, and we were shot up into the midst of them; the Deputy followed in a car. Once again we were in the open; it was about 2 am, a fine cold night, and not a sinner to be seen on the deserted North Circular Road. We made as much noise as we could, singing, etc, and as we rounded the corner of Prussia Street, and saw a group of men near the market, we shouted 'Up the Republic'. The men took off their hats and shouted with us. We called to them that we were Republican women prisoners being taken from Mountjoy to the North Dublin Union, but we were soon out of sight and hearing; we saw no more wayfarers, and finally pulled up at our destination.

Sinn Féin protests against Free State executions, 1923

Sinn Féin survives the Civil War

In June 1922, Republicans had won 36 seats in the General Election held in the 26 Counties. Another General Election was held in August 1923. Despite the fact that Republicans had been ruthlessly repressed and thousands were in jail, Sinn Féin contested, as described here by Máire Comerford:

Máire Comerford

Enormous numbers of our people were in jail, about 11,000 of them. We had no machine to fight it. The Free State was riding high and sure of winning. The organisation gave me a motor bike, and gave me the whole of Cork to organise for Sinn Féin, except Cork City. It was a herculean task. Only one of our TDs in Cork was at liberty, Daithi Ceannt. He lived in the wilds of East Cork and survived only by staying out of sight. I had the greatest difficulty making contact with him. The motor bike was unable to reach Castletownbere because of the high wind. Nearly all 36 of our TDs were on the run. De Valera appeared once on a platform in Ennis. It was fired on by Free State troops, and he was arrested. I was arrested myself in Fermoy, and brought to Cork Jail and lodged there. William Cosgrave immediately directed that I be released…

There was mass intimidation too on election day. Dozens of our people manning polling booths were arrested... Our booths were completely unmanned and there was no one to watch the count. Nevertheless, despite this strange exercise in democracy by the Free State, Sinn Féin did well in the election. Our seats went up from 36 at the 1922 'Pact' election to 44 in this first all Free State election of 1923. I was thrilled and felt grateful to the people.

Arrest of de Valera in Ennis, County Clare, 1923

Partition of Ireland entrenched

The provision in the Treaty for a Boundary Commission led many to believe that it would make the 'Northern Ireland' state unworkable. However, the report of the Commission in 1925 left the Border largely unaltered. The Free State Government signed an agreement with the British on 3 December guaranteeing the whole of the Six Counties to the Unionist Government under the Crown.

Republican TDs' declaration against Partition

In the name of the Irish nation and the Irish race, in the name of all who have stood and will yet stand unflinchingly for the sovereign independence of Ireland, we, the duly elected representatives of the Irish people, by our names appended hereto, proclaim and record our unalterable opposition to the partitioning of our country...

Despite repression from the Free State Government, Sinn Féin successfully fought the 1923 election

The Nationalists of Fermanagh are overwhelmed with amazement that any men representing the country can sign such a document. It is a betrayal of the Nationalists of the North and a denial of every statement put forward by the Free State in their alleged support of our case since 1921... The Parliament of the Six Counties has been given additional powers in the cancellation of the Council of Ireland without any guarantee that this power will not be used for the persecution of large Nationalist majorities in the Border areas... John Redmond was driven from public office for even suggesting partition for a period of five years. The new leaders agree to partition forever.

Free State parliament spurns Northern Nationalists

The agreement with the British was debated in the Free State parliament on 9 and 10 December after a request by Northern Nationalist representatives to address the assembly was turned down. One of the few TDs who spoke against the agreement was Richard Corish of Labour. The agreement was ratified.

I am absolutely opposed to this Agreement, because I consider that the Executive Council have exceeded their functions in the matter. I consider that the Government has gone as far as to break the Constitution; I consider that the Government has gone as far as to break the Treaty which they have been praising for the past three or four years. Deputy Dr. MacNeill, who was appointed by the Government as a member of the Boundary Commission, told us two or three weeks ago, in the greatest confession of failure I have ever heard a man make, that he pledged himself to secrecy with two men whom he knew very early in the proceedings were absolutely opposed to the aims of the Free State. He told us that early in the proceedings of that Commission it was clear to him that his colleagues were not putting a proper interpretation on the Article in question. I do not care what his conception of honour may be; I believe that he should, there and then, have told them that he considered it his bounden duty to come back and tell this country of that. The honour of Deputy Dr. MacNeill is a very small thing compared with the future of this nation. The honour of Deputy Dr. MacNeill, great as he may think it is, is a very small thing compared with what the Nationalists of Tyrone and Fermanagh have gone through and will go through.

The formation of Fianna Fáil

Sighle Bean Uí Dhonnchadha
(Sighle Humphries)

At an emergency Sinn Féin Ard Fheis on 9 March 1926, Eamon De Valera proposed the ending of abstention from Leinster House once the Oath of Allegiance to the British monarch was removed. This was narrowly defeated and De Valera and his supporters departed from Sinn Féin to form Fianna Fáil. Sighle Bean Uí Dhonnchadha was a Cumann na mBan activist and here describes what followed:

Fianna Fáil might not have entered Leinster House in the way they did in August 1927 but for the Electoral (Oath) Act, brought in that summer, whereby candidates had to give an undertaking that, if elected, they would attend. I remember listening to De Valera speaking in Tralee upon the economic situation in 1925. He was magnificent when he urged us on to buying Irish, but there was no applause for him. Then he said: 'I know you are all wondering if we will enter the Free State parliament. As long as water flows, we will never go in. Our business is to stand fast and firm. And fast and firm we shall stand, even if we are reduced to the last man.' Within a few months, however, they were on their way in. Must politics be so devious?

We lost very few Cumann na mBan to Fianna Fáil then, except Madame Markievicz. It nearly broke our hearts to lose her. We did not even want to accept her resignation, which, under our constitution, we were obliged to do. Alas, nobody won her, she was dead within a year.

Saor Éire

Saor Éire was an initiative by the IRA to mobilise workers and small farmers in support of republican and socialist goals. Its emergence, and that of other republican groups and campaigns of the '30s came about as Fianna Fáil swept up the republican vote. Sinn Féin became increasingly marginalised, with its adherence to a rigid interpretation of abstentionism isolating it even from other republican organisations. This is from the first (and only) National Congress of Saor Éire in Dublin in September 1931.

Saor Éire is the mobilisation of the militant workers and working farmers who realise that the overthrow of imperialism demands the exposure of the role of the Irish industrialists fighting for greater freedom in the home market. It demands the mobilisation of the Irish people in conflict with native exploiters who are the allies of British imperialism. The freedom of Ireland can only be achieved by the mass of the Irish people so mobilised and realising the goal towards which they must struggle is an Irish Republic, based on the possession and administration by the working farmers and wage-earners of the land and instruments of production, distribution and exchange, and that the cleansing of Ireland of British Imperialism involves the abolition of the inhuman and degrading social system.

The IRA and Fianna Fáil

The groundswell of opposition to the Free State Government of W.T. Cosgrave swept Fianna Fáil to power in the General Election of 1932. Many IRA members actively supported Fianna Fáil in that campaign. They did so after the Army Council suspended an order forbidding Volunteers from working or even voting at elections in either the Six or the 26 Counties. In January 1932, the IRA Army Council issued the following order to its units:

The Army Council made the following decisions:-

(a) That the order be suspended which forbids Volunteers to work or vote at elections for membership of the so-called Northern Ireland or Free State parliaments.

(b) That in the pending election in the 26 Counties Volunteers and supporters are recommended to vote against the candidates of the Cumann na nGaedhal party and other candidates who actively support the policy of that party.

(c) That while Volunteers and supporters are recommended to vote it must be clearly understood that Óglaigh na hÉireann do not accept or approve of the policy of any of the parties contesting the elections.

(d) Volunteers shall not become candidates nor shall they speak on the platforms of any of the parties.

It is strongly recommended that the Election campaign be availed of for the holding of meetings in every unit. At these meetings the policy of Óglaigh na hÉireann shall be put before the people from our own platforms.

Realising the natural urge to end the rule of a party which has been responsible for so much national disaster and economic distress, the Army Council would, however, emphasize to Volunteers that while advocating voting at these elections, our objects cannot be achieved by the methods or policies of the parties seeking election...

IRA Chief of Staff
Maurice Twomey

Republican women, including Maud Gonne MacBride (right), protest on O'Connell Bridge, Dublin

BOYCOTT BRITISH GOODS

PRISONERS OF EMPIRE 5,000 WOMEN IN INDIA

Republican Congress,
Shankill Road contingent,
Bodenstown, 1934

Republican Congress

Frank Ryan was a leading member of the IRA, and former editor of its weekly paper, An Phoblacht, *who departed with others such as Peadar O'Donnell and George Gilmore to form the Republican Congress in 1934. Gilmore later stated that the Congress was "an effort to free the republican-minded people of Ireland in the trades unions and in the countryside generally from the illusion that Fianna Fáil leadership was leading towards their freedom in Ireland and to set them to work on what can be called a Tone-Connolly approach to their emancipation". While Congress itself split shortly after its formation, it did much to highlight the plight of working people, such as this from its newspaper edited by Ryan:*

The slums of York Street

We, the people of York Street, Dublin, living in tenement rooms, considering the assistance your paper has given in publicising the true facts of these cases, and the assistance given by Republican Congress, request you to publish the conditions of our living accommodation...

Some of our tenants are practically condemned to death in the basement cellar, front and back kitchens, some of which are already condemned by the Corporation authorities. We are paying weekly rents of 7 shillings for each of these apartments; no air or sunshine can enter these cellars...

The sewerage traps, some placed on the floor of the kitchens, continually burst open when heavy rains come, and all the contents of the sewerage is emptied into the basement. Swarms of rats are a constant worry to us, and as many as thirty rats have been caught in one kitchen in one week; they even devour the birds swung from their cages in the centre of the ceiling... Countless millions of bugs have infested several of the rooms in the area, and we are in constant bodily pain and our little children can get no natural sleep from the torture of this vermin and day by day they are growing weaker...

The 1937 Constitution

In 1937, De Valera put his new Constitution to a referendum. For the period of the referendum campaign the ban on the republican newspaper, An Phoblacht, *was lifted and the paper campaigned against the adoption of the new Constitution. On 15 May 1937, it carried the following manifesto and report of a rally — the second in two nights — which was held despite a ban by the Fianna Fáil Government.*

Manifesto from Republican Organisations

We, the undersigned, on behalf of Irish Republicans, call on the people of Ireland to repudiate the latest Free State political manoeuvre – the "Constitution of Éire" – because:

1. It is not the Constitution of the Republic of Ireland. The word Republic is not even mentioned.
2. It holds this ancient nation partitioned as a 26-County British Dominion and a 6-County British Crown Colony whilst British garrisons continue in occupation North and South.
3. It does not end Partition.
4. It does not end the evils of Imperialism in Ireland and, like its predecessor of 1922 which was imposed by force of arms by renegades and traitors, it is a negation of the Republican principles for which our bravest and best have given their lives.
5. We re-assert on behalf of the Nation that Republican Ireland will not compromise on the National position, and we call on the people not to relax their efforts until the political, economic and social independence of Ireland is achieved.

Signed, Tom Barry
Signed on behalf of Cumann na mBan — Eithne Coyle (President)
Signed on behalf of Sinn Féin — Mrs. Buckley (President)
Signed on behalf of Mná na Poblachta — Sheila Grennan (President)
Signed on behalf of Cumann na Poblachta — D. O'Riordan (President)

When Tom Barry, his head swathed in bandages as a result of batoning in the previous night's fighting, mounted the platform a number of police, led by an Inspector, attempted to come towards the platform, but angry shouts and the pressure of determined men against them, made them retreat. The crowd by this time filled Cathal Brugha Street and extended out across O'Connell Street, 5,000 would be a meagre computation.

Barry was received with tremendous enthusiasm. For several minutes he could not speak; the crowd were cheering, calling "Up the IRA", "Up Kilmichael".

"The Free State Government has banned the Republican demonstration last night, but they failed to prevent it," Barry declared. "It was held in spite of them..."

Frank Ryan, who was also given a rousing welcome, then addressed the meeting. He pointed out that the attempt by the authorities to prevent the people of Dublin from expressing their loyalty to the Republic had failed. In spite of proclamations and police savagery, meetings had been held and Republicans had paraded the streets. He spoke of the pleasure it gave him to be associated once again with the men on the platform, especially Tom Barry... Whatever else the New Constitution might be it certainly was not the Constitution of an Irish Republic, nothing short of which would ever satisfy the Irish people – Ireland united, Ireland free, Ireland a Republic governed by the plain people.

Margaret Buckley on poverty in Ireland

Margaret Buckley was elected President of Sinn Féin in 1937, a position she held until 1950. At the Ard Fheis of 1938 she described the dire social and economic conditions in the Ireland of the 'hungry '30s'. Margaret Buckley was also a leading member of the Irish Women Workers' Union.

The outward semblance of prosperity created by the streets lined with motor cars; the crowded cinemas; the highly powered new lighting system, poised on standards of foreign manufacture, is only by way of contrast to the poverty and demoralisation which is hidden away in places, not so well lighted; and the hopelessness and helplessness which is eating into the souls of decent men and women who are denied the right to work, and whose moral fibre is being undermined by doles and idleness. Men and women stand idle in the market place, while little girls and boys, who ought to be still at school become the family breadwinners, in factories which multiply monthly, in basements and other unhygienic places, shut out from even the light of day....

Margaret Buckley, Sinn Féin President, 1927-1950

The rich become richer and the poor become poorer; emigration is greater than ever, as it is easier to raise the fare to England than to America; our rural areas are becoming denuded and depopulated; soon there will be no Irish Nation left...

Na hÉireannaigh sa Spáinn ar son na Poblachta

Chuaigh na céadta poblachtánaigh Éireannacha chun an Spáinn idir 1936 agus 1939 chun troid ar son na Poblachta. Thacaigh an tAthair Mícheál Ó Flanagáin, Uachtarán Sinn Féin idir 1933 agus 1935, leis an Phoblacht. Seo sliocht as cumhní cinn a scríobh Eoghan Ó Duinnín a throid sa Spáinn i 1938.

Níos faide ar aghaidh d'fhágamar an bóthar; thosaíomar ag dreapadóireacht. Ag tarraingt go hanróiteach in aghaidh an chnoic dúinn, ní fheadfainn gan smaoineamh ar abairt a raibh Peadar O'Donnell an-tugtha dó sna tríochaidí - the high ground of the Republic. Ní raibh aon easpa maidir le talamh ard san tír máguaird. San áit seo a bhí las zonas más elevadas de la región.

Chuamar suas, duine i ndiaidh duine. Bhí na piléir agus na slogáin ag teacht tapa go leor - na slogáin ag pléascadh rófhada uainn chun aon díobháil a dhéanamh. Ní raibh an raon ceart acu go fóill. Tar éis tamaillín, nuair a bhíomar cóngarach do bharr an chnoic, chonaiceamar corp anseo agus ansiúd. An chéad mharbhán a chonaic mé (sínte ar thaobh an tsléibhe) bhí sé ina luí ar a aghaidh, a dhá géag sínte amach aige ar an talamh - fear ag ligean a scíthe, cheapfaí. Bhí beirt fhear i ngar dó agus chuala mé duine díobh a rá: 'Thug mé rabhadh dó i dtaobh an bhuidéil uisce sin atá aige gan clúdach'. De réir cosúlachta. Bhí an ghrian ag taitneamh ar mhiotal an bhuidéil agus cuireadh piléar díreach tríd. Múrach, is dócha - b'iontach na haimsitheoirí iad.

Proinsias O Riain (tríú duine ar chúl)
le Oglaigh Poblachtánacha sa Spáinn

Deaths in prison

The short-lived and ill-fated IRA bombing campaign in England in 1939 met with a massive backlash from the Free State, Stormont and British governments. Republican political activity once again centred on support for the prisoners. In England, Peter Barnes and James McCormick were hanged in February 1940, in spite of an international campaign for reprieve. In April, Tony D'Arcy of Galway and Seán McNeela of Mayo died after a hunger strike against criminal treatment in Mountjoy Prison. This leaflet was issued after D'Arcy's death and before that of McNeela:

Another Day Gone

Tony D'Arcy, Irish Republican Prisoner, after hunger strike of over 7 weeks, has died. The lives of other Republican prisoners, also on hunger-strike for over 7 weeks, are drawing to a close. They have used this form of protest as the only one possible to obtain the age-old object – political treatment. Not for themselves, observe, but for those of their comrades who have been degraded as common criminals.

"Greater love no man hath" – Would to God that all Irishmen had their loyalty, tenacity and courage.

"Far dearer the grave or the prison
Illumed by one patriot name
Than the trophies of all who have risen
On Liberty's ruin to fame."

Tony Darcy, brave Soldier of the Republic, has died.

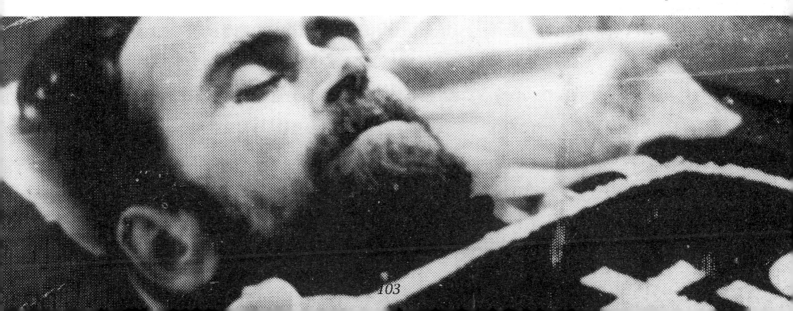

Among the Republican prisoners dying in Irish jails on 7 weeks' hunger strike are veterans of the National struggle for the past 30 years, some of them sentenced to death in 1916. Where the British failed to achieve De Valera is going to succeed and send Jack Plunkett to a felon's grave beside his martyred brother, the poet, Joseph. That is if the community continues to look on in dumb-founded silence.

Irish People, have you forgotten your heritage so soon!

Open the Gates!

The execution of Tom Williams

Tom Williams

IRA Volunteer Tom Williams of Belfast was hanged in Belfast Prison, Crumlin Road, on 2 September 1942. Five others had been sentenced to death with him but were reprieved. One of them, Joe Cahill, recalls the day of the execution.

I had been moved to A Wing by this time and our special Mass was at half-past eight. The thing that struck me that morning was the terrible silence in the prison. I have a vague recollection of that awful, eerie stillness being broken only when I heard snatches of Orange songs, party songs, being sung outside the prison.

At half-past eight the doors were opened and we headed up to the prison chapel, still in complete silence. The only sounds to be heard on the way to the chapel were footsteps and sobbing, hundreds of men sobbing over the loss of a comrade. Father McEnaney celebrated the Mass. Sitting in the front row along with us, the long-term prisoners, were Father McAllister and Father Alexis.

Father McEnaney was in such a state that he was not able to complete the Mass. Towards the end he was emotionally overcome and Father Alexis said the final prayers from his position off-altar...

I was in A1 and in the cell above me was a guy called Kevin McQuillan. Around twelve noon he rapped the floor and shouted, "Joe, quick, get up to your window." From my cell window I could see a gap between A Wing exercise yard and B Wing. You could look straight across to the hospital. What we wanted to see was Tom's funeral heading towards the grave at the back of the hospital. Warders were carrying Tom's coffin and the three priests were with them. They were out of sight in a few seconds...

"Clare speaks to De Valera"

On 11 May 1946, Seán McCaughey died in horrific conditions on hunger and thirst strike in Portlaoise Prison. Three days before his death, people in Co. Clare issued this appeal.

To: An Taoiseach, Eamon de Valera TD.

We the people of the historic parish of Inch, in meeting assembled, do hereby call on you as head of the Twenty-Six County Government and our Senior Deputy, to release forthwith and unconditionally, Seán McCaughey and his fellow Republican prisoners...

You seem at the moment to be drunk with power, and believe that the people have become so debased that their support is assured to you. Have a care, Basil Brooke and Co. are doubtful bed-fellows. If you follow in their footsteps much further your 1921 wish to be buried in a Fenian grave will never be realised. Of a surety if the people are ever as deluded as to attempt burying your remains in a Fenian plot, the dead Fenians will arise in their wrath and eject you out of it.

Funeral of Seán MCaughey passing through the centre of Dublin, May, 1946

Funeral of Seán Sabhat,
O'Connell St, Dublin, 1957

106

Resurgence

1949-1962

Protestant Republican honoured in Christ Church Cathedral
Republican resistance re-emerges
National Unity and Independence Programme
Daring Armagh raid
Two prisoner candidates elected
Resistance campaign begins
Sinn Féin banned by Stormont
Seán Sabhat agus Fergal O'Hanlon
Four Sinn Féin TDs elected
Internment North and South
Edentubber
Sinn Féin organiser murdered
End of Border Campaign

Protestant Republican honoured in Christ Church Cathedral

By 1948 the rebuilding of the Republican Movement was under way and in May of that year its new monthly newspaper, The United Irishman, *was launched. In September, the bodies of six Republicans executed by De Valera between 1940 and 1944 were released from prison graves and reinterred with full honours by the Republican Movement. Two of them were the Protestant Republicans George Plant of Tipperary, and 1916 veteran Patrick McGrath of Dublin.* The United Irishman *describes their funerals:*

These funerals have also proved another thing, that the Republican Movement is not a sectarian movement. It embraces Irishmen of all religions and of all classes. Paddy McGrath the Catholic, and George Plant the Protestant, died bravely for the same cause, the cause of the Irish Republic...

Proudly the funeral procession marched on its way past the General Post Office, through Westmoreland Street, into College Green, where Pearse had reviewed the Volunteers on St. Patrick's Day, 1916, just a month before the Rising, on up Dame Street to Christ Church Cathedral where the bell was tolling as the funeral procession passed the City Hall. It was nearly half-past eight when the funeral reached Christ Church. A halt was made, and General Plant's body was lifted from the hearse and carried into the Cathedral. This was indeed an historic occasion. A Protestant soldier of the Republic was being received with full military and ecclesiastical honours in the capital city of Ireland and for the first time in history the Irish Tri-Colour entered Christ Church Cathedral, covering the body of a Republican martyr.

Inside Christ Church, after the remains had been carried to the High Altar, the IRA Guard of Honour once again took up its place around the coffin and two Ministers read the Service...

Republican resistance re-emerges

In June 1951, the IRA, of which the public had heard little for several years, carried out a raid on Ebrington Barracks in Derry, capturing a cache of arms and ammunition. This resurgence coincided with a visit to the Six Counties by members of the English royal family and protests by Sinn Féin, as The United Irishman *reported:*

Then came the incidents arising out of the visit of members of the English Royal Family to inspect their "loyal subjects in Ulster". Arrangements were made by the Seán McCaughey Cumann in Belfast to hold a protest demonstration and meeting on the night of Thursday, 30th May, and posters advertising these events were put up on Saturday 26th, but were torn down or defaced by the RUC.

In the early hours of Tuesday morning, 28th May, large-scale raids were made on the Republican houses of Belfast and thirteen men were arrested and thrown into Crumlin Road Jail without charge or trial. Among them were Jimmy Steele and Liam Burke, recently released after long years in jail. In spite of the raids and arrests, and the police interference with their publicity, the protest demonstration was held on Thursday night as arranged. A parade formed up in Hamill Street, and headed by two Tricolours, marched up the Falls Road to Clonard Street, where an enthusiastic meeting was held. Speakers included P. McCotter, chairman, Tom Heenan, S. Ó Cearnaigh, C. Ó Murchadha, Tomás Ó Dubhghaill and S. MacCriostal. One last kick by the RUC was the intimidation of the owner of the lorry and of the loud-speaker hirers. Of course the 'Nationalist' Press were too careful or too loyal to carry advertisements for the meeting...

National Unity and Independence Programme

In 1954, the Ard Chomhairle of Sinn Féin, which then had its headquarters in Abbey Street, Dublin, issued its National Unity and Independence Programme. Sinn Féin stood two abstentionist candidates in the Leinster House General Election — Martin Whyte in Clare and Joe Campbell in Louth and summarised the four main points of the Programme in this address to voters:

Election Address to the People of Clare and Louth

In asking you to vote for Sinn Féin we are asking you to declare the right of the Irish people to separate nationhood and independence.

The Sinn Féin candidates in the 1954 General Election stand by the same principles and programme held by Tone, Emmet, Mitchel, Fintan Lalor, the men of the '16 period and later, men like Tony D'Arcy, Charlie Kerins and Richie Goss.

While all Irishmen applaud this principle, the Republicans in Sinn Féin and the other branches of the movement — IRA, Fianna Éireann and Cumann na mBan — are determined, with the co-operation and help of the people of Clare, Louth and all Ireland, to use ALL the means advocated and used by these men, who have proved they are the only effective means to force English power out of Ireland.

Separation means complete freedom for the Irish people to work out the life of the nation in all its political, economic, social, cultural and other aspects without interference from any foreign power. The Republican Movement, through Sinn Féin, proposes

1. To convene the elected representatives of all Ireland as the National assembly of the Independent Irish Republic.
2. To proceed to legislate for all Ireland.
3. To use every means within the power of the Irish people to overcome opposition to the Republic.
4. To repudiate all treaties, pacts and laws that in any way curtail the nation's independence...

Daring Armagh raid

The IRA raided Gough British Army Barracks in Armagh City in June 1954, capturing a large consignment of weapons. The United Irishman *editorialised:*

When the news flashed in great headlines across the newspapers, when it was repeated on the radio, Irish shoulders straightened, Irish heads lifted higher and there was a feeling of delight everywhere. In the public streets, in factories and workshops, in the theatres and dance halls, the mention of Armagh brought rounds of applause. Men who were active republicans but who have since grown tired, men who have been Free State supporters since 1922, men who "never took part in politics", all echoed their praise of the courage and daring of the lads who carried it out.

For all are agreed on this one point that the British Army has no right in Ireland — it is the army of the aggressor, of the robber Empire, and its only right in Ireland is the right of conquest, of naked force. Even Irishmen who themselves had served in the British Army agree that it has no right here and that it must be got out. This is what gave rise to the feeling of delight at Armagh — not the capture some guns, though that is important, not to make the British Army look foolish, not merely a spectacular operation, but to emphasise the fact that the British Army of Occupation is still in Ireland, that it holds Irish territory by force of arms and that it must be cleared out.

Two prisoner candidates elected

In May 1955, Sinn Féin fielded 12 candidates in the Westminster elections in the Six Counties. Tom Mitchell was elected in Mid-Ulster and Phil Clarke was elected in Fermanagh/South Tyrone. Both Dublin men, they were among five Dubliners and three Corkmen captured and sentenced after an IRA raid on Omagh Barracks the previous November. The British Parliament unseated Mitchell because he was a convicted prisoner. A by-election was held in August and Mitchell won again. An Election Petition Court was held and Mitchell was unseated again. Mitchell was taken under armed guard from Crumlin Road to Omagh for the hearing. The intervention of a second nationalist candidate in the subsequent second by-election allowed the Unionist to win.

Address of Tom Mitchell, Sinn Féin MP for Mid-Ulster, to
Election Petition Court, Omagh, October 1955

We all know that this Court has on trial today the people of Mid-Ulster — the trial having taken the form of an election petition... My main reason for coming here is that it is right I as a representative of Mid-Ulster should state their views. When the obvious result of these proceedings is announced it will mean that the majority of the people of Mid-Ulster have been disenfranchised.

I am proud to be the representative of this area, the more so because I come from Dublin and until the people of Mid-Ulster decide otherwise I will hold myself as their representative... Instead of taking my seat at Westminster, we asked the people to return us to the 32-County Parliament which I hope will be attained some day and will be a full Dáil Éireann. This policy was obviously accepted in view of the fact that myself and Phil Clarke were elected by the Republican people of the Six Counties, who turned out in force to elect us.

The British Government sought to interfere in the case and unseat me. A by-election was called and the people made a very forceful reply to this travesty of democracy and returned me this time with a triple majority... What the British government failed to accomplish is now being accomplished by this petition under British law...

Resistance campaign begins

The IRA opened a new military campaign — 'Operation Harvest' — in the Six Counties on 12 December 1956 with attacks on British barracks and other installations. The following rallying call was issued by Sinn Féin on 16 December and read at public meetings throughout the country on that day:

Irishmen have again risen in armed revolt against British aggression in Ireland. The Sinn Féin organisation states to the Irish People that they are proud of the risen nation and appeal to the people of Ireland to assist in every way they can the Resistance Movement in the Six Counties.

Over the past 35 years, all constitutional means have been tried by the Irish people to free themselves from British occupation. Even where a constitutional programme got the full support of the people, their will was invalidated by British courts. It was obvious that the young men of this generation would have to rise as the young men of other generations have risen against such tyranny.

Constitutional methods alone against armed occupation, civil injustice and victimisation could not possibly be made effective. Only when Ireland is completely free and independent will Ireland be at peace.

Sinn Féin appeals to the Irish people to support Sinn Féin policy — the establishment of an All-Ireland Parliament, unfettered by any outside power.

Is sinne
Máire Ní Ghabhann
Micheál Tréinfir.

Sinn Féin banned by Stormont

One of the first reactions of the Unionist government in Stormont to the IRA's Resistance Campaign was to ban Sinn Féin. The United Irishman *reported in a special bulletin in January 1957. The ban on Sinn Féin in the Six Counties remained in place until 1974.*

The main opposition to the Stormont regime in the Six Counties is provided by Sinn Féin. At the last Imperial election Sinn Féin candidates polled one third of the votes cast in the Six Counties.

Stormont decided to wipe out this opposition and in the process wipe out Sinn Féin. Without any public announcements it banned Sinn Féin during the last week of December.

Sinn Féin headquarters in Belfast was raided and the office equipment confiscated. Sinn Féin election workers throughout the North have been interned.

A Sinn Féin Céili, scheduled for Strabane on New Year's Night, was banned by order of Colonel Topping, the Stormont Minister for Home Affairs. Also in Strabane, an Irish language class attended by more than 100 people was banned.

Sinn Féin election rally, 1957

113

The funeral of Seán Sabhat; (inset): Fergal O'Hanlon (left) and Seán Sabhat (right)

Seán Sabhat agus Fergal O'Hanlon

Maraíodh Óglaigh Seán Sabhat (Luimneach) agus Fergal O'Hanlon (Muineachán) in ionsaí ar bheairic an RUC ag Brookeborough, Co. Fear Manach, 1 Eanáir 1957. Ghlac na mílte páirt ag na sochraid. Diarmaid Ó Donnchadha a labhair cois uaigh Sabhait i Luimneach.

Ba mhór aige prionsabail, ba mhór aige saoirse, ba mhór aige Gaelachas. D'éag sé ar son na saoirse, ar mo shonsa agus ar bhur sonsa, agus ar son na nglún atá le teacht. Ní hamháin gur lean sé lorg Mhic Piarias agus Emmet agus Tone, ach dhein sé staidéar ar dhúchas agus stair Gael ó thosach ré na staire - agus dhein sé beart dá réir. Chuir sé amach dhá eagrán de Ghath, agus in alt a bhí san eagrán deiridh scríobh sé Jacta alea est, nó más fearr leat an Ghaeilge, 'Ta deireadh le raiméis! Tá ré na cainte thart!' Bhí deireadh le caint agus ráiméis fad a bhain siad le Seán.

Ach an fíor go bhfuil deireadh le raiméis? Níor mhian liomsa aon duine a fheiceáil anseo innniu ach an duine atá sásta lorg Sheáin a leanúint. Bíodh a bheatha agus a bhás ina dteagasc agus ina dtreoir dúinn. Is minic a chualathas le tríocha bliain anuas ráiteas úd an Phiarsaigh: 'Saor agus Gaelach'. Tá a fhios ag an saol cad a dhein Seán ar son na saoirse. Tá a fhios againne a raibh aithne againn air cad a dhein sé ar son na Gaeilge. Ní labhródh sé riamh aon fhocal Béarla. Bíodh sin ina threoir againne.

Irish-Americans picket the British consulate in New York, 1958.

Four Sinn Féin TDs elected

In the 26-County General Election of March 1957, four TDs were elected for Sinn Féin — Eanachán Ó hAnluain (Monaghan), Ruairi Ó Brádaigh (Longford/Westmeath), John Joe McGirl (Sligo/Leitrim) and John Joe Rice (South Kerry.)

Sinn Féin Election Address 1957

The politicians of all parties have brought our country to the verge of disaster. They have had ample time to implement their policies over the last 35 years, yet the legacy they pass on to us of a new generation is pitiful indeed; England's stranglehold on the industrial North-East is unbroken; the Gaeltacht is dwindling year after year; a quarter of a million of our youth and bloom lost in emigration over the last five years alone; 95,000 unemployed in the 26 Counties and 40,000 in the Six Counties. Ireland literally "lies broken and bleeding", while we are burdened with taxation to maintain two States and three Governments...

Internment North and South

The Stormont regime in the Six Counties had imposed internment without trial at the start of the IRA campaign in December 1956. De Valera's Fianna Fáil Government followed suit. The members of the Ard Chomhairle of Sinn Féin were among the first interned when they were arrested at Ard Oifig, 31 Wicklow Street, Dublin on 6 July 1957. The United Irishman editorialised:

Mr. Erskine Childers was busy telling a Longford audience that his government was prepared to fill every jail and barracks in the country with Sinn Féiners! On the face of it that seemed an indiscreet remark for some days earlier Mr. De Valera has declared that none of the arrested members of Sinn Féin (including the President and Ard Chomhairle) was jailed for membership of Sinn Féin! Mr. De Valera might do worse than recall the old axiom that when English politicians praise an Irishman's actions he should examine his conscience to see what he has done wrong.

John Joe McGirl who was
elected Sinn Féin TD for
Sligo/Leitrim, 1957

Mr. De Valera has received plenty of praise from British sources over the past few months. And the Irish people — who at no time gave Fianna Fáil a coercion mandate — might ponder these questions: will the Curragh Concentration Camp advance our demands for unity and independence? Will it solve our national and economic problems?

Edentubber

On 11 November 1957, five Irish Republicans were killed in an accidental explosion at Edentubber on the Louth-Armagh border. They were Oliver Craven (Newry), George Keegan (Enniscorthy), Patrick Parle (Wexford), Paul Smith (Bessbrook) and Michael Watters (Edentubber). Sinn Féin Sligo/Leitrim TD John Joe McGirl spoke at the funerals of Craven, Smith and Watters who were buried in the Republican Plot in Dundalk cemetery.

John Joe McGirl TD at Edentubber funerals

The tragedy which brought to a sudden end the lives of these five great Irishmen is a tragedy of the Irish nation. The tragedy of an Ireland that is unfree and divided. These men came from North and South to join together to end the tragedy of our nation and her people.

Michael Watters was symbolic of the mass of the Irish people who have borne the brunt of the struggle for Irish freedom... For 35 years the Nationalists of the North looked to their brother Irishmen in the South for a direct lead against British Occupation. They were sadly disillusioned by the inept approach to the problem of Occupation by their fellow Irishmen in the South. Having examined and explored all peaceful approaches to the unnatural division of our country they once again asserted their God-given right to freedom and have fought side by side with gallant comrades from the South...

Sinn Féin organiser murdered

James Crossan, Sinn Féin organiser for County Cavan, was shot dead by the RUC in the early hours of 24 August 1958, on the Cavan-Fermanagh border. A pamphlet on the murder published by Sinn Féin questioned the conclusions of the inquest which found 'justifiable homicide' after the RUC claimed that Crossan and others were preparing to attack a customs post and ran away when challenged.

James Crossan

Why did no member of the patrol involved give evidence as the inquest? The only evidence came from a Head Constable who knew nothing about the shooting until one hour after it is alleged to have occurred. If James Crossan was shot down near the Customs Post why did it take two hours to discover his body?...

If he was called on to halt a number of times and did not and since the area involved was extremely close to the Border surely he would have escaped across the Border by the time the patrol opened fire? If he was shot by a burst from a Sten gun, it is well known that the effective range of this weapon is very close — possibly less than 50 yards. Medical evidence was that James Crossan was shot on the right hand side of the chest. The bullet was found in the body. There was no exit wound. The bullet must have entered the body from the front. If he was running towards the Border at the time and away from his pursuers why was he shot in the chest?

We suggest the whole Crown case is a very clumsy effort to cover up a murder.

End of the Border Campaign

The IRA's campaign had dwindled by the end of 1961. In the 26-County General Election of that year, Sinn Féin lost all four seats it had won in 1957. The end of the armed campaign in the Six Counties was announced.

The leadership of the Resistance Movement has ordered the termination of the Campaign of Resistance to British Occupation launched on December 12, 1956... Foremost among the factors motivating this course of action has been the attitude of the general public whose minds have been deliberately distracted from the supreme issue facing the Irish people — the unity and freedom of Ireland...

For over five years Irish freedom-fighters have fought against foreign occupation, native collaboration and the overwhelming weight of hostile propaganda. Supported loyally by the Republican people of the Six Occupied Counties they have faced fantastic odds. 5,000 British regular troops, 5,000 territorials, 12,500 B-Specials, 3,000 RUC, 1,500 specially trained Commandos and sundry security guard forces — totalling close on 30,000 armed men — bar the road to freedom...

Terroristic tactics against the civilian population, draconian laws, imprisonment without charge or trial, torture-mills to force 'confessions' from prisoners, long and savage penal servitude sentences, the shooting down of unarmed people at roadblocks and threats of even sterner measures including flogging and hanging have all been employed to maintain British rule in the Six Counties...

The Curragh Concentration Camp was opened and maintained for close on two years with 200 uncharged and untried prisoners. When public opinion forced its closing down, the Prisoners' Dependants Fund was attacked and hundreds of collectors jailed. When this tactic too was defeated, proceedings against Resistance fighters and their supporters at 26-County District Courts were suspended by the introduction of a Military Tribunal in November last...

During the five-year campaign over 600 operations against enemy patrols, strong-points, communications, transport and civil administration have been carried out at enormous cost to the enemy... The Resistance Campaign is in a position to continue its campaign in the occupied area indefinitely. It realises, however, that the situation obtaining in the earlier stages of the Campaign has altered radically and is convinced that the time has come to conserve its resources, to augment them, and to prepare a more favourable situation... The Irish Resistance Movement renews its pledge of eternal hostility to the British Forces of Occupation in Ireland. It calls on the Irish people for increased support and looks forward with confidence — in co-operation with the other branches of the Republican Movement — to a period of consolidation, expansion and preparation for the final and victorious phase of the struggle for the full freedom of Ireland.

Signed:
J. McGarrity
Secretary
Irish Republican Publicity Bureau
February 26, 1962.

Former members of Cumann na mBan at a National Graves Association reunion 1960s

RUC confronts Civil Rights marchers

Civil and national rights
1962-1970

Wolfe Tone bicentenary

The year 1963 marked the bicentenary of the birth of Theobald Wolfe Tone. The Wolfe Tone Society — later renamed Munitir Wolfe Tone — was established to apply Tone's principles of unity to the Ireland of the 1960s. The Northern Directory of the Society included a number of Republicans from a Protestant background. Journalist Jack Bennett was one of them and he edited a special one-off souvenir newspaper, Wolfe Tone Today. *This is from the editorial:*

We believe that the Irish nation springs from a fusion of people of a variety of racial origins as a result of their sharing an exclusive common history upon the common territory of Ireland.

We believe that Pict and Gael, Danish and Norman invader, English and Scots settler have all blended in the crucible of history into one vigorous and resourceful people with its own distinctive characteristics — characteristics which, while varying in places, set the Irishman recognisably apart from other peoples...

We declare that it is a self-evident falsehood to state that there are two nations in Ireland. We believe that even the Orangemen, in the very nature of their dispute with fellow Irishmen, are talking politics which are Irish politics alone, and of no consequence, and of very little interest, to any other nation...

The Stormont administration, set up by Act of Parliament of another nation to manage local affairs, exists solely by grace of another nation's parliament, and is an administration bereft of all normal governmental powers except those concerning the ordinary administration of local services. It is not a government at all, but is an administrative convenience through which another nation exercises its rule over Irish territory...

Máirtín Ó Cadhain

Scríobhneoir i nGaeilge agus Óglach Poblachtánach ab ea Máirtín Ó Cadhain (1905-1970). Bhí sé sa Churrach sna 40í. I 1963 thug sé léacht do Mhuintir Wolfe Tone agus seo thíos sliocht as.

Is iad Óglaigh na hÉireann an dream is faide is mó a d'fhulaing ar son na hÉireann, is mó a thur seirbhís d'Eirinn, dá bhfuil beo anois. Rinne siad gan luach saothair, gan aon tsúil le luach saothair é. Ba bheag de lucht réabhlóide na hÉireann go dtí iad féin nach raibh ómós an phobail orthu as ard nó as íseal. Ach lean siad lorg na laochra. Dhá suaraí an té a fhéachas le é sin a dhéanamh, ligeann sé cuisle rúnda laochais eicínt ann féin. An t-oifigeach Gearmánach Goertz a tháinig anseo le linn an Choga is beag dea-fhocal a bhí aige do na hÓglaigh. Ach tá amhdaithe aige pé ar bith cé an locht a bhí orthu nó nach raibh, nár casadh aon duine acu leis a ghlacfadh airgead uaidh ar mhaith len a leas féin.

Sé Tone ár bpátrún. Sé a chuimhneachán an druileáil faoi rún, an phríosúntacht, na stailceannaí, na troideannaí, na báis óna lá féin go dtí an lá inniu. Ní raibh an ghlúin seo ar deire mara raibh sí chun tosaigh. Níl bliain ó 1923 nach ndearnadh rud eicínt leis an troid sin a chothú, a choinneáil ar bun: troid in aghaidh na Léinteachaí Gorma, troid in aghaidh an Tuaisicirt, in aghaidh Shasana i Sasana, in aghaidh an Tuaiscirt sa Tuaisceart. Bhí na cúirteanna speisialta éigeandála, na campaí géibhinn agus na príosúin, na téarmaí saoil, éalaithe, stailceannaí, an chroich, na báis....

Tá an comhraic sin ó '23 cho síoraí seasta le aon chomhraic i stair na hÉireann. Rinne an ghlúin seo a gcion féin den imirt thaibhseach ar a dtugtar gaisce coga. Bhí bearaic Ard Mhacha in 1954 ar shaighdiúireacht cho maith is a rinneadh in Éirinn ó Sheachtáin na Cásca...

Máirtín Ó Cadhain ag labairt ag agóid de chuid Cumann Cearta Sibhialta na Gaeltachta, 1969

Loyalists burn Bombay Street, August, 1969

The Tricolour and the election — Gerry Adams enters politics

Sinn Féin was still banned in the North in 1964 but it contested the Westminster elections in all 12 constituencies in the Six Counties, with its candidates described as 'Republican'. The Unionists won all 12 seats. The 'Republican Clubs' were formally established the following year. In 'The Politics of Irish Freedom' Gerry Adams describes an event that had a deep influence:

During the Westminster elections in October 1964, rioting occurred after a Tricolour was displayed in the window of Sinn Féin's election office in Divis Street in Belfast. Ian Paisley objected loudly to the display of the flag and threatened to march on Divis Street and remove it within two days if it hadn't been removed by then. The next day a force of RUC men broke down the door of the office and removed the flag. Two days of intense rioting followed and the republicans, accompanied by a large crowd of local people, replaced the flag, only to have it removed again by RUC men wielding pick-axes. Three hundred and fifty RUC men using armoured cars and water-cannon and wearing military helmets launched an attack on the Falls and 50 civilians and 21 RUC ended up in hospital. The government had responded to pressures from Paisley and had provoked a violent reaction from the Catholic working class. It was a stark reminder of where the balance of power lay in the Six Counties.

I was in school at the time but the Divis Street events concentrated my mind on politics. I already possessed a vague sense of discontent and the naked display of state violence against the people of the Falls made me feel I did not want merely to stand by looking on. I found myself spending a few evenings in the Felons' Association rooms on the Falls Road folding election material for Liam McMillan, the Sinn Féin candidate. Despite, or maybe because of, all the republican candidates losing their election deposits, within a few months I joined Sinn Féin.

Séamus Costello at Bodenstown '66

Séamus Costello took part in the '50s campaign, was wounded and interned. On release he quickly became a key figure in both Sinn Féin and the IRA. His oration at Bodenstown in 1966 was regarded as confirmation of the Republican Movement's increasingly socialist orientation. He remained with the leadership of Cathal Goulding and Tomás MacGiolla after the split of 1969/70. Having broken with them to form the Irish Republican Socialist Party and the Irish National Liberation Army in 1974, he was assassinated by the so-called 'Official IRA' in 1977.

We must aim for the ownership of our resources by the people, so that these resources will be developed in the best interests of the people as a whole. Some of you may feel that these aims are impossible to achieve until such time as we have an independent all-Ireland government. It is certainly true that some of these aims will not reach fruition until such time as we have an all-Ireland parliament. However, in the meantime, you as republicans have an extremely important part to play in the furtherance of this policy.

It is your duty to spearhead the organisation of a virile co-operative movement among the farming community. It is also your duty to use your influence as trade unionists to organise a militant trade union movement with a national consciousness. In short, it is your duty to become active, hard working members of each and every organisation that is working for the welfare of all the people and towards the reunification of the country.

You should use every possible opportunity to acquaint the people with our policies on land, industry and finance. We believe that there should be a limit to the amount of land owned by any single individual. We also believe that the large estates of absentee landlords should be acquired by compulsory acquisition and worked on a co-operative basis with the financial and technical assistance of the State.

In the field of industry, our policy is to nationalise the key industries with the eventual aim of co-operative ownership by the workers. The capital necessary to carry out this programme can be made available without recourse to extensive taxation by the nationalisation of all banks, insurance, loan and investment companies whose present policy is the re-investment of our hard-earned money in foreign fields...

The lesson of history shows that in the final analysis the robber baron must be disestablished by the same methods he used to enrich himself and retain his ill-gotten gains, namely, by force of arms. To this end we must organise, train and maintain a disciplined armed force which will always be available to strike at the opportune moment.

Civil Rights Movement takes to the streets

The Civil Rights Movement, formally organised as the Northern Ireland Civil Rights Association, began in 1967 when a range of individuals and organisations came together to formulate basic demands for change in the sectarian Orange state. Many of them were Republicans, including members of the Wolfe Tone Societies. They demanded one person, one vote in all elections, an end to the gerrymandered local government boundaries, an end to discrimination in the allocation of housing, an end to discrimination in employment and the repeal of the repressive Special Powers Act. The First Annual General Meeting of NICRA was held in February 1968 and began a series of protests, culminating in the march in Derry on 5 October 1968 which was attacked by the RUC at Duke Street. TV footage of protestors being batoned were shown around the world and escalated the political crisis for the Unionist regime. Fergus O'Hare and Geraldine Holland later recalled the background to '68:

There were many factors which came together to produce the upsurge which occurred in 1968. There were international factors such as the struggle of the Vietnamese people to win their freedom and the international campaign which was built up around the struggle demanding that US troops be withdrawn. There was the struggle for civil rights for black people in the USA and events such as the Paris uprising of that year. All of these played some part in creating a consciousness among people here, particularly young people, of the power of mass protests and demonstrations.

There were economic factors. The decline of traditional industries in the North led to the raising of hopes among nationalist workers that the patterns of discrimination that had existed in the old unionist-controlled industries might change. When these hopes were not realised nationalist resentment was fuelled.

There were social factors such as the existence for the first time of fairly large numbers of middle-class Catholics, who had benefited from the availability of free education, and who wished to stake a claim for themselves in the northern statelet. They saw their opportunities to advance within the North being thwarted by the continuation of discrimination.

There were political factors such as the raising of nationalists' hopes for a better deal by the talk of reforms from the new 'liberal' unionist Prime Minister at Stormont, Terence O'Neill. But when his much talked of reforms failed to materialise once again nationalists felt justifiably aggrieved.

But while all these factors played an important role in creating the circumstances which made the events of 1968 possible it must be remembered also that for several years prior to '68 the grievances of the nationalist community had been exposed and explained not only in the North of Ireland but in the 26 Counties and further afield. For more than four years organisations such as the Campaign for Social Justice and the Campaign for Democracy in Ulster had been highlighting injustices against the nationalist community in the North.

The Belfast pogrom

While the Battle of the Bogside raged in August 1969 in Derry, the B-Specials were mobilised in Belfast. Loyalist mobs and B-Specials attacked nationalist districts and the narrow streets between the nationalist Falls Road and loyalist Shankill Road became a scene of conflagration. Loyalists burned nationalist Bombay Street to the ground. During July, August and September 1969, 1,505 Catholic families and 315 Protestant families left their homes in Belfast. British troops were deployed throughout the North. Nationalist Archie Livingstone recalled his experience:

When I got back to Divis Street I could see there was trouble. I was stopped from getting to our house in Dover Street by my son Pat who was then about 16. There was a barricade across Dover Street and young people were fighting off a large number of loyalists which was gathered at the other end. Pat said, "There's a couple of shots after being fired down the street, Da. Follow me and we'll get to the house." He brought me back to the house via Boundary Street. Bernadette, my wife, had the front door barricaded and the kids were terrified.

We went upstairs to look out the window. The loyalists had invaded the nationalist end. They were led by B Specials and by Councillor Johnny McQuade, Paisley's man, who was in the middle of them giving orders.

The Sarsfields GAA Club was the first to go up. Then they started to break the windows. There was 16 of a family in Tohill's next door to us. Their house was fire-bombed. Then they broke our parlour window and in came petrol bomb after petrol bomb. Nothing could have put the flames out.

Bernadette and I and and the kids fled for our lives over the back wall which was covered in glass. Julie was then aged two. We got into the council yard. Several times we tried to get across the road into Divis Flats but the RUC from Hastings Street Barracks were firing up the street. We had to dodge our way across the street to get to the flats. We lost everything, our home, all our clothes. And that was the start of the Troubles.

Sinn Féin splits

The leadership of the IRA under Chief of Staff Cathal Goulding and the leadership of Sinn Féin under party President Tomás Mac Giolla sought to drive through fundamental constitutional, strategic and tactical changes in the Movement's direction within a few short years from about 1965 onwards. This alienated many members. Some left the Movement. Many remained and opposed the leadership. By December 1969 the divisions had crystalised around the lack of preparedness of the IRA for events in the Six Counties. When the Sinn Féin Ard Fheis assembled in the Intercontinental (now Jury's) Hotel in Ballsbridge, Dublin, on 10 January 1970, the IRA had already split and a Provisional Army Council had been established. The Goulding leadership failed to win the required two-thirds majority to change the Sinn Féin Constitution to allow participation in the Westminster, Stormont and Leinster House parliaments. They then put a motion pledging allegiance to the IRA leadership that had already abandoned the abstentionist policy. Almost half the delegates walked out on Sunday 11 January and reconvened at Kevin Barry Hall, 44 Parnell Square. There they elected a Caretaker Executive of Sinn Féin, headed by Ruairi Ó Brádaigh. They issued a detailed statement on 17 January setting out their position, extracts of which are carried here:

Seán Mac Stiofáin, second from right, who led the Provisional Army Council in 1969 IRA split, pictured in Free Derry. Left to right, Martin McGuinness, Daithi Ó Conaill and Seamus Twomey

Cathal Goulding

Where Sinn Féin Stands

We believe that the delegates who 'walked-out' had long been disgusted with the internal methods in operation in the Movement for some time and indeed with the general atmosphere at the Ard-Fheis... In Belfast, three Republican Clubs were denied representation on the grounds that they had been 'inactive' since August last. We leave it to the public to assess the validity of this last subterfuge, bearing in mind the circumstance of Belfast for the past six months. It seems hardly likely that any Republicans would be inactive. In all this harassment of the delegates opposed to 'recognition', many of the full-time paid officials of the organisation were unduly active...

Let Down of North

Despite repeated warnings from last May on, sufficient priority was not given to this matter, with results too well known to require enumeration. The leadership of the Movement was obsessed with the Commission and getting its recommendations adopted and preparations for the defence of our people did not receive the necessary attention. We will not dwell at length on this matter since it is self-evident to any observer of the Northern scene. We might add that we feel particularly strongly on this point.

We find absolutely incomprehensible from any Republican stand-point the campaigning in favour of retaining the Stormont parliament in August, September and October last when it was in danger of being abolished altogether by the British Government. In any future struggle for freedom it would surely be preferable to have a direct confrontation with the British Government on Irish soil without the Stormont junta being interposed. In any event, the taking away of the Orange Order's power-bloc would surely be a step forward rather than backward...

Many of those who left the Intercontinental Hotel and went to Parnell Square have worked hard in Housing Action Committees, the National Waters Restoration League, Land Leagues and such like and will continue to do so. We believe in the need for an Economic Resistance Movement to arrest the decline and take-over of our country and we will continue on constitutional lines to organise the people to achieve our objectives of Irish freedom, political, economic, social and cultural...

We have played, and will continue to play, our part in the struggle for Civil Rights in the Six

Counties. We believe in vigorous local government representation and we have the support of the majority of Sinn Féin local councillors in our present stand. We seek to build an alternative 32-County state structure which will draw off support from the existing British-imposed partition system within which our objectives are unattainable.

A number of assumptions and impressions exist in the public mind due to speculative and inaccurate reporting:

(a) That we are militarists who will promote 'border raids' is untrue. We will, nonetheless, support all efforts to defend our people in the Six Counties.

(b) It is said that we are 'wild men', whose policies are crude and old-fashioned, while those now in opposition to us are reasonable people. To this we reply that while we adhere to basic principles we believe in forward-looking policies as has been outlined in this statement.

(c) The generalisation that those who intend recognising Westminster, Stormont and Leinster House are 'progressives', while we are 'traditionalists' is also false. They will at best end up in parliamentary blind alleys as have other splinters from the Republican Movement — Cumann na nGaedheal (now Fine Gael), Fianna Fáil and Clann na Poblachta, not to mention the Northern Nationalist Party. This was the British intention in imposing the 'settlement' of 1921 and after 50 years the constitutional framework has failed and frustrated the Irish people. While we take our inspiration and experience from the past we are realistic as to what will strengthen the people's will to resist British imperialism and what will weaken that will. Participation in the institutions designed to frustrate our people's progress to full freedom is certain to weaken that will to resist...

Sinn Féin President, Ruairi Ó Brádaigh

We have the support of Republicans in almost all the country outside of sections in Dublin and Wicklow and a small number of scattered individuals elsewhere. We are going ahead and one of our steps is the launching of a new Republican monthly newspaper which will be called AN PHOBLACHT, the first edition of which is expected on February 1st.

For a number of years now those involved in the take-over have traded on the good name of Sinn Féin — a name respected for honesty, integrity, sincerity and national ideals by Irish men everywhere. Now that that umbrella has been removed from them, they stand exposed and the Irish people in their own way can now form their judgement.

We are content to leave it at that.

Joe Cahill and
Dáithi Ó Conaill

Defiance at Bodenstown

The reorganised Republican Movement assembled at Bodenstown in June 1970. The oration was given by Dáithi Ó Conaill.

To the British Government we say this: You stand indicted before the world for the wrongs you have done in Ireland. You never had any right to be in our country and you never will. You sent your troops to keep what you call the peace. You forget that peace must be based on justice; it cannot be founded on British bayonets. The more your troops impose their will, the nearer you bring the day of open confrontation. If you sincerely desire peace, then withdraw your armed force and the weapons of destruction you so lavishly supplied to the Stormont junta over the last 50 years. In a nutshell, get the hell out of our country; you never brought us anything but strife and war.

The defence of Short Strand

Jim Gibney

On 27 June 1970, armed loyalists attempted to over-run the nationalist district of Short Strand. The defence of the district by Volunteers who gave allegiance to the Provisional Army Council was widely seen as a key moment in the rebirth of the IRA. Short Strand native Jim Gibney, later a key figure in the development of Sinn Féin, recalled that night as he witnessed it:

He emerged, carrying an object, which looked like a rifle of some sort. He walked awkwardly to the corner of the street like a man not used to carrying such lethal weapons. Excited and shocked by what I was watching my brain registered these events and for a split second I was recording in slow motion my first ever encounter with a man carrying a gun.

He had hardly passed me 'til the screech of gunfire tore the tranquil evening apart. Rapid bursts of gunfire, then screams of "Fenian bastard", which in turn elicited "Orange bastard"... Then more bursts of gunfire. Torn between fascination and fear I placed one foot in the hallway and another on the street and watched...

I crept, hugging the walls of the houses for safety, to the end of the street where I joined two snipers with their faces blackened who regularly fired at people as they petrol-bombed the chapel precincts or menacingly ran past a street junction 100 yards away. Two loyalists walked coolly into the path of their gunfire. I watched them casually light a petrol bomb and hurl it over the convent wall before walking into Duke Street. The snipers, numbed by their audacity, paused momentarily but then fired at them as they disappeared unharmed...

A scene of devastation greeted the bleary eyes of Sunday morning Mass-goers; burnt out buses zig-zagged across streets; pubs, the centre of community entertainment for decades, smouldered in heaps of rubble; the sexton's house, a few yards from the chapel, lay in ruins. The chapel's doors bore scorch marks, testimony to the intensity of battle. A local man, Henry McElhone, was dead; another, Billy McKee, an IRA man, was badly wounded.

I later learnt I was witness to a chapter in the district's history where similar events had been enacted on many occasions, in those same streets, for over 50 years.

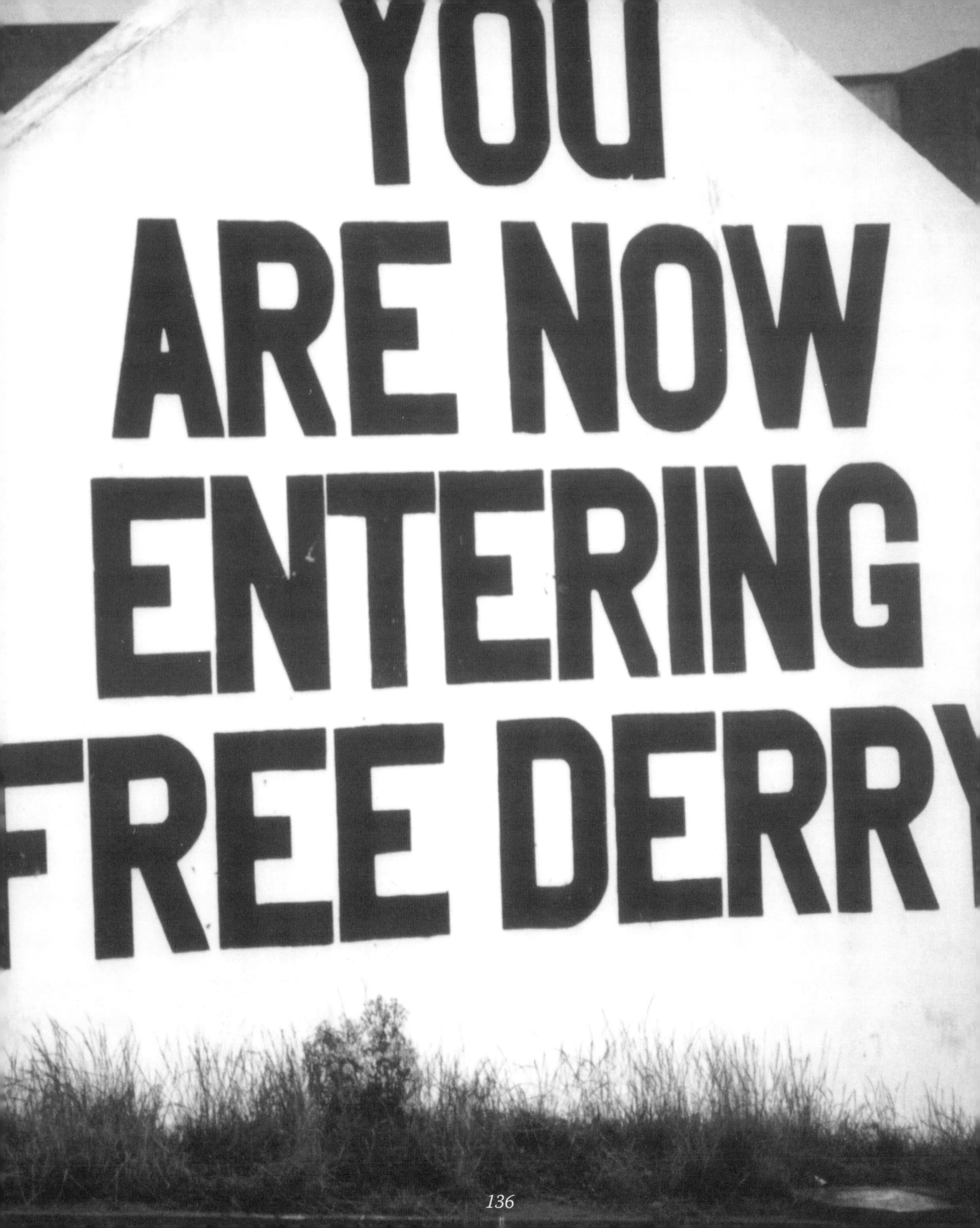
YOU
ARE NOW
ENTERING
FREE DERR

The risen people

1971-1975

Internment without trial
Bloody Sunday
Over 20,000 at Bodenstown '72
The British Army unleashed
Sinn Féin offices closed by Fianna Fáil government
The Bill and the Bombs
President jailed
Littlejohns meet An Phoblacht editor in Mountjoy
Éire Nua
Brutality in Long Kesh
Michael Gaughan
The burning of Long Kesh
Máire Drumm rallies the nationalist people
Proinsias Stagg
Sinn Féin Vice-President murdered

Internment without trial

Internment without trial was imposed by the British Government in the Six Counties on 9 August 1971. It was to remain in place until 1975 and in that period over 2,000 people were interned. One of them was People's Democracy activist and writer John McGuffin, whose book 'Internment' (Anvil, 1973), became a classic of Irish prison history. McGuffin was himself 'lifted' in the first internment swoop, as he describes here:

In the early hours of Monday 9 August 1971, I was kidnapped from my bed by armed men, taken away and held as a hostage for five and a half weeks. I was not in Uruguay, Brazil, Greece or Russia. I was in the United Kingdom, an hour's flight from London. I was in Belfast.

A crashing on the door awoke me. It was 4.45 o'clock. I went down the stairs in my pyjamas to answer. As I opened the door I was forced back against the wall by two soldiers who screamed at me "Do you live here?" Overwhelmed by their perspicacity I admitted that this was so, whereupon they ordered me to get dressed. I foolishly asked why. "Under the Special Powers Act we don't have to give a reason for anything," an officer said. "You have two minutes to get dressed." Through the window I could see in the dawn light half a dozen armed men skulking in our tiny front garden.

British Army Internment swoop, August, 1971

ELIZABETH THE FIRST

Inset left: A paper cutting from 1971 calling for the release of the first woman internee, Liz McKee

Internees flown to internment camps by RAF helicopter

I was given exactly two minutes to get dressed while a young soldier boosted his ego by sticking an SLR [rifle] up my nose. My wife, not surprisingly, was almost in tears as I was dragged down the stairs and into the street...

"Tie him up and gag the fucker," an educated English accent ordered. "That's hardly necessary," I said, as I was frisked a second time up against a lorry or 'pig' as they called it...

My name was called. Apprehensively I shuffled forward. I was taken by two young Special Branch officers who identified themselves — the only ones to do so during my four interrogations — into a room and desultorily questioned. They obviously knew very little about me and cared even less. Names, address, occupation (lecturer) and a few general comments such as "Well it's at least five years for you." What interested me more was the view past them through the window. On the lawn outside, the helicopter stood, engines still revving and blades rotating. A dozen or so barefoot men were being forced to run the gauntlet between two rows of military policemen who were clubbing them with sten-gun butts and batons. Those who fell were badly kicked. When they reached the helicopter they were grabbed in and then thrown out again almost immediately. The noise of the helicopter drowned any screams.

The interrogators noted my concern. "That's nothing to do with us," one said. "That's just the army letting off a bit of steam."

Bloody Sunday

The Derry march of 30 January 1972 was planned as a revival of the Civil Rights Movement. Its primary focus was the demand for the end of internment without trial and it was hoped that a return to the streets could provide a political avenue amidst the rising military activity. But the actions of the British Army, who killed 14 unarmed civilians, were to escalate the conflict further, making 1972 the worst year in terms of death and injury. One of the most striking accounts of Bloody Sunday is that of Fulvio Grimaldi, the Italian photographer who took many of the most famous images of the massacre and whose book, 'Blood in the Street', was published in March 1972. Here he describes the death of Kevin McElhinney, aged 16:

In the middle of the yard a small body, with outstretched arms, face to the sky, head to the Flats. Like on the cross. Under the hail vomited by the filthy insects, heroes come to life and to unforgettable memory. A first aid boy, in the uniform of his duty, in the spirit of his love. Kneeling near the body, lifting the head gently: white, thin face framed in black, a young boy's face, as clean as the early sky, as empty of life. Eyes slowly fading away, back into himself. A priest crawling towards the two, and then another man.

I wave a white handkerchief and go to the group. Get down on my knees, want to see, pale face, half-open mouth, eyes back into himself, whiter, whiter still, tattered pullover, poor boy's pullover, slipped up, white chest, fragile, vulnerable, white skin, skin of a living boy, skin without blood gradually, chest without air, slack, thin stomach, caving in, poor boy's stomach, delicate, weak. I see between the shoulder of the priest and the first aid man, see like through a pipe because of the two leaning over Kevin, or perhaps because I am looking through the reflex, to see better, to make you all see. Never to forget. To know what to do. To them. The murderous sub-humans. The soulless mechanical tools. And their masters, the mad, frothing, mad scientists.

The priests kneels. He raises his right hand. He drops it. His mouth is strained like in a forced smile. He weeps. He raises his hand again and draws a cross over Kevin, weeping.

I didn't know then. I now remember that it was then and there that I changed the film. Automatically. Subconsciously obeying through the means of experience and conditioned reflexes the one imperative: keep going. At least beat them by one photograph. One more picture than bullets.

The men lift Kevin in their arms. There is a hole in the back of his thigh and one in his shoulder. The same bullet. The sort of ammunition one would use for elephants.

The priest raises a white handkerchief which drops with blood saying: Kevin is dead, Kevin has been killed by you. Now let us through. Wrath bigger than any fear of monster, however nightmarish. Now death is with us. We have it in our arms. Nothing can hurt us any more. Not all those bullets buzzing over our heads, past our ears.

A perfect opportunity for whoever exists in a condition where the values of life and death, of love and destruction, have been turned upside down. A great occasion for the mechanical insects. As the group gets going towards the entrance of Chamberlain Street the firing livens up. Perhaps they don't want to kill us now, just a little scare. We may as well know that a dead boy means nothing to insects. Whether he has a clean face and a vulnerable little chest or not...

The priest bends down and keeps his bloody handkerchief high, the others proceed at his side. The bullets keep getting directed at us. The priest bends lower, hankie still high, goes into a crouch, handkerchief on the ground to support him. The bullets fly lower. Then suddenly, before being finished like worms crawling on the ground, we all get up together, straight, forward. And are invulnerable. A scream, unbelievably loud: "You see now what the British Army is like?"

Over 20,000 at Bodenstown '72

The massive growth in support for Irish Republicanism after Bloody Sunday was shown at Bodenstown where An Phoblacht *estimated that over 20,000 attended. The speaker was Seán Keenan of Derry, whose son Volunteer Colm Keenan had been killed on active service the previous March.*

There is a new spirit in Ireland that cannot be ignored. It has destroyed a Government that but a few short years ago seemed firmly established. Stormont is gone and the monolithic Unionist party recently all-powerful is now making protests reminiscent of the Stormont opposition for the past 50 years...

We should rid ourselves of the notion that the Six Counties should come into the 26 and think that Ireland, divided for 50 years, is to be united.

The Constitution which will govern a united Ireland must be worked out by the people of Ireland and put to them for acceptance or rejection. Meanwhile all groups in the South must make plain that they are willing to have a non-sectarian Constitution, making a start to convince Protestants of their good faith...

No people deserve peace more than Republicans. No people suffered more in every decade since Stormont was set up. We want to see an end to internment. We want the young men on the wanted list able to move through the streets without danger of being shot down. We want true peace. We want freedom first. Let us pledge ourselves that we will continue the fight until our country is free.

RUC on the rampage in Derry

Littlejohns meet *An Phoblacht* editor in Mountjoy

Kenneth and Keith Littlejohn were London criminals who were recruited as agents by British Intelligence. They operated in the 26 Counties and carried out bank robberies, attacks on Garda stations and other operations designed to discredit the IRA. The editor of An Phoblacht, *Eamonn MacThomais was jailed in 1973 but continued to write a column from Mountjoy Jail. Here he describes meeting the Littlejohns:*

I first met Kenneth and Keith Littlejohn on Friday, August 3rd. It was in the reception room of Mountjoy Jail, where we were being searched and handcuffed before being brought together to Green Street Courthouse...

At first I thought they were two Special Branch men. They were dressed to kill and looked like the whizz-kid type of Branch man in Dublin Castle. But then I heard their names mentioned and saw the handcuffs coming. Before leaving the reception room I had found out details, names and addresses of other British agents and the full inside story. They both spoke freely — yet were afraid I might attempt to kill them. "It's a good job you're handcuffed," they said. "You have your side, we have our side. You're Irish, for Ireland; we're British, for England. I'll bet you have your spies too."

Kenneth did most of the talking. We went back over the same ground of how they made contact with the British Government. They told of the plan to push the Dáil into passing the repressive legislation against the IRA and of the bank raids to discredit that organisation. The idea was to open up the way for internment without trial and they spoke of the fear of the British Government that the war in the North would be taken to the streets and cities of England.

They told me of their meetings with Wyman at the Burlington Hotel and of the role of Crinnion and other Special Branch agents who were (and are still) on England's payroll. They told me how they had got the names and addresses of the top Republicans from the Dublin Castle files.

Repub
arriva
an are

Eamonn MacThomáis, editor of An Phoblacht, just prior to his arrest at 44 Parnell Square, 1973

Sinn Féin activist Marie Moore addressing a public rally in Belfast, 1970's. On the right is Belfast Republican Liam Hannaway.

Sinn Féin poster

Éire Nua

In 1973, internment without trial continued and there was intense repression by the British Army in nationalist areas of the Six Counties. The nationalist 'no-go' areas had been invaded by the British Army in Operation Motorman in July 1972. As well as this policy of repression the British Government initiated talks designed to establish an administration involving the Unionists and the Social Democratic and Labour Party (SDLP). This culminated in the Sunningdale Agreement in November 1973 in which the section of Unionism led by former Stormont Prime Minister Brian Faulkner agreed to lead a new Executive involving the SDLP and the Alliance Party. Sinn Féin at this time was boycotting all the elected institutions in protest at internment. It put forward as its alternative the Éire Nua programme which called for a Four Province Federal Ireland.

The object of the Republican Movement is to establish a new society in Ireland — Éire Nua. To achieve that aim, the existing system of undemocratic Partition rule must be abolished and replaced with an entirely new system based upon the unity and sovereignty of the Irish People. The new system shall embody three main features:

(1) A New Constitution
(2) A New Governmental Structure
(3) A New Programme for Social and Economic Development.

The New Constitution would provide:
(a) A charter of rights which would incorporate the principle of securing to the individual protective control of his conditions of living subject to the common good.
(b) A structure of government which would apply this principle by providing for the maximum distribution of authority at provincial and subsidiary level.

The proposed government structure would be federal in character and would consist of four levels:
(a) Federal (Central) Government: based upon the unity and sovereignty of the people of Ireland.
(b) Provincial Government: based upon the four historic provinces.
(c) Regional (Administrative) Government: based upon clearly defined economic regions.
(d) District (Local) Government: which would replace existing local government North and South...
The establishment of Dáil Uladh would be the first step towards the creation of this new governmental structure for the whole island. By thus creating a Provincial Parliament for the nine counties of Ulster within a New Ireland, the partition system would be disestablished and the problem of the border removed. Dáil Uladh would be representative of Catholic and Protestant, Orange and Green, Left and Right. It would be an Ulster Parliament for the Ulster people. The Unionist-oriented people of Ulster would have a working majority within the Province and would therefore have considerable control over their own affairs. That power would be the surest guarantee of their civil and religious liberties within a New Ireland.

Brutality in Long Kesh

Internees in Long Kesh were held in Nissen huts within barbed wire compounds. Assaults on the prisoners were commonplace. Internee Brian Rafferty described one such assault in May 1974:

At approximately 5am on Tuesday 14 May I was awakened by the noise of British soldiers who were shouting at the entrance to the hut where I was sleeping. They then charged down the length of the hut hitting lockers and beds with their batons and at the same time screaming orders for us to obey immediately...

I was being dragged out of my bed by a group of soldiers and was being beaten and kicked by them. They were battering me over and over again. I don't know how many times I was hit, but anyway after the first dozen or so blows I could not feel anything more.

Somehow I managed to get to my feet and to my horror I saw my brother Charles being batoned by a group of soldiers. They were hitting him over and over again on his back and head.. I asked him how he was feeling and he mumbled something about being hurt bad. I saw that he was almost collapsing so I moved over to him and held him steady At this point he blacked out and fell to the ground. I asked one of the soldiers for a doctor and I was told there would be no doctor brought for an Irish bastard and furthermore if I didn't get up against the wire again they would send the dogs up for us...

In Long Kesh.

Front row: Tom Cahill, Tommy Toland, Gerry Adams

Back row: Jimmy Gibney, Tomboy Loudon, Brendan Hughes, Terence 'Cleeky' Clarke, Bobby Sands

Last message

Proinsias Stagg died on 12 February 1976. This was his last message to the leadership of the Republican Movement:

We are a risen people. This time we will not be driven into the gutter, even if this should mean dying for justice. The fight must go on. I want my memorial to be Peace with Justice.

Hijacking of Stagg's body

The Fine Gael/Labour Government of Liam Cosgrave was determined to prevent another public demonstration of respect for an IRA hunger striker as seen at the funeral of Michael Gaughan. They hijacked the body of Proinsias Stagg to prevent the Republican funeral which he had requested. The Garda Special Branch buried his body under concrete in Ballina. Sinn Féin mobilised thousands of people in the town on 22 February and held a ceremony to honour the hunger striker. Joe Cahill gave the oration. Stagg was reburied in the Republican Plot beside Michael Gaughan later that year.

Today we are assembled here under strange and morbid circumstances to pay honour and homage to one of Ireland's bravest and best soldiers. Strange and morbid not by our actions but by the actions of those who have aligned themselves with the ancient enemies of Ireland.

Today it was our intention that we should stand by the graveside of Proinsias Stagg but that is denied us by the ghoulish actions and body-snatching tactics of Quislings. Actions which will be seen and judged by the world to be deeds of deranged, demented and defeated men. Perhaps it would be better to say animals. Actions of people who have failed to learn from the past. Have they forgotten the lessons of the B Specials or the RUC?

Sinn Féin Vice-President murdered

Sinn Féin Vice-President Máire Drumm was murdered by loyalist assassins in her bed in Belfast's Royal Victoria Hospital on 28 October 1976. The Republican Prisoners paid tribute to her:

On Thursday 28 October 1976, Roy Mason, the British Secretary of State for the 6 occupied counties of North East Ireland, stated in the British House of Commons that he was examining ways of dealing with the 'Godfathers and Godmothers', the instigators of violence.

What in reality he was saying was that the British were desperately trying to find some way to further repress the revolutionary struggle of the Republican Movement against British imperialism in Ireland. That night, within hours of Mason's speech, Mrs. Máire Drumm, a prominent member of the Republican Movement and an outspoken critic of British interference in Irish affairs, was shot dead. As yet no group has admitted responsbility and even if some obscure loyalist faction should claim that they carried out the assassination, there can be no doubt in our minds that Mrs. Drumm's death can be directly attributed to the British Government.

If they believe that killings such as this will intimidate Republicans from carrying on the war for national liberation they are very much mistaken. Mrs. Drumm's courage and determination to end British domination of Ireland has been in the past an inspiration for Republicans to continue the struggle until the last vestiges of British imperialism in Ireland have been torn down.

To Mrs. Drumm's family and relatives and many, many friends we extend our deepest sympathy. To the British , the cause of her death and of our nation's ills, we pledge unceasing opposition.

Republican women in Belfast defy British ban on hurleys. Máire Drumm is on the right.

157

Gerry Adams (left) at the funeral of an IRA Hunger Striker, 1981

The long war

1976-1991

British not withdrawing
British try to suppress news of H-Blocks
Torture in Castlereagh
IRA unbeaten
National H-Block Committee established
Women in the New Ireland
The Hunger Strikes of 1980 and 1981
Bobby Sands elected MP for Fermanagh/South Tyrone
Death of Bobby Sands
Plastic bullet deaths
Dublin establishment spurns prisoner TDs
RTÉ censors Prisoners' MP
The Hunger Strike ends
Electoral strategy under way
First election breakthrough in Six Counties
Adams takes West Belfast
38 break out of H-Blocks
Adams elected President of Sinn Féin
Forum's 'bag of dolly mixtures'
The Hillsborough Agreement
Abstentionism from Leinster House dropped
A Scenario for Peace
Republican funerals attacked by RUC
Loughgall
Enniskillen
March '88 — month of tragedy
Sinn Féin/SDLP talks
British broadcasting ban
Ireland's 'Berlin Wall'
Nelson Mandela calls for Irish peace talks
Political extradition
Revisionists answered
Collusion targets Sinn Féin members

British not withdrawing

At Bodenstown in June 1977 the oration by Jimmy Drumm was significant as setting the direction for Republicans in the years ahead. Many had believed that the British Labour Government was seriously contemplating withdrawal from the Six Counties. Cabinet papers since released show that this option was indeed considered but was never a real possibility at that time. It would mean a long road for Republicans:

We need a positive tie in with the mass of the Irish people who have little or no idea of the sufferings in the North because of media censorship and the consolidation of conservatism throughout the country. We need to make a stand on economic issues and on the everyday struggles of the people

Jimmy Drumm

The British Government is not withdrawing from the Six Counties and the substantial pull out of businesses and closing down of factories in 1975 and 1976 were due to world economic recession though mistakenly attributed to symptoms of withdrawal. Indeed the British Government is committed to stabilising the Six Counties and is pouring in vast sums of money to improve the area and assure loyalists, and secure from loyalists, support for a long haul against the Irish Republican Army. So sectarianism is to be maintained and increased repression of the Nationalist population with the aid and backing of the Free State administration are what lie ahead.

By 1977, while the IRA retained support in national[?] areas, it was clear that Britis[h] withdrawal was a long way o[ff]

British try to suppress news of the H-Blocks

By April 1978, the H-Blocks of Long Kesh had been open for two years and the British criminalisation policy was in full swing. All Republicans convicted after 1 March 1976 were treated as criminals, even though their comrades in the nearby Cages of Long Kesh, convicted prior to that date, retained political status. Sinn Féin and the Relatives' Action Committees now stepped up their campaign for the prisoners, many of whom had been tortured by the RUC, before sentencing in juryless Diplock courts. On 22 April 1978, Republican News carried a special supplement reporting on conditions in the H-Blocks. The RUC response was to carry out mass arrests of Sinn Féin members, to raid Republican News offices and printers and to seize copies of the paper. This piece is from the supplement they tried and failed to suppress:

Britain's concrete monument of shame

300 'Blanket Men' are brutalised daily

Every minute of every day of every week these men suffer

- No clothes — only a blanket to clutch around them with bare feet on concrete floor.
- No association — either kept in solitary confinement or two to a cell built for one; these men only leave their cells for 45 minutes per week to go to Mass.
- No exercise period — those who try physical exercises in their cells get exhausted very quickly due to lack` of proper food, lack of fresh air and lack of normal exercise
- No bedding for three days — every fortnight their bedding is removed from the cells during the day for three days; and the men are sentenced to 14 days loss of remission.
- No proper food — no food parcels allowed; all food is served stale and cold in small, revolting portions....

Protest now — before one of these heroic men is brought home in a box.

Political status for Republican Prisoners.

Women protest in support of Armagh Prison Hunger Strikers, 1980

First blanket man released

The first participant in the blanket protest in the H-Blocks of Long Kesh was Kieran Nugent. He was released in May 1979 and welcomed at a public rally organised by Sinn Féin in Belfast. He described how he began the protest and the motivation of his comrades:

When in Crumlin Road jail on remand I realised the need to oppose the criminalisation policy inside the jail. With a few other lads I discussed the best way. I didn't know at that time that the protest would involve a blanket. I decided not to wear a prison uniform because it distinguished the criminal status prisoners from political prisoners.

On Friday I left behind my comrades still struggling for their rightful recognition as political prisoners. Their words to me were, 'Tell the people we cannot be with them today because we are prisoners of war but we are with them in spirit.'

This protest is not about conditions or privileges. It is about the right of political prisoners to be recognised as prisoners of war, a war declared by the British Government itself.

Political status is not a privilege which the British Government can take away. It is our right as combatants in the war of national liberation.

Kieran Nugent, the first blanket man, welcomed on his release at a Belfast rally with Tom Hartley of Sinn Féin

Torture in Castlereagh

As well as campaigning for the prisoners in the H-Blocks, Sinn Féin at this time was also highlighting the torture of detainees in RUC interrogation centres, most notoriously, Castlereagh outside Belfast. This is a typical report from An Phoblacht/Republican News *in August 1979:*

Emmanuel Cullen was first arrested seventeen months ago in February 1978, when he was only fifteen and a half. On that occasion, mainly because of his age, the RUC held him for less than 20 hours. However, as was reported in *Republican News* at that time, he was beaten and he was threatened with arrest again, when he reached the age of 17. The RUC, true to their threat, arrested him two weeks ago, the day following his 17th birthday.

During his incarceration in Castlereagh he was interrogated on six separate occasions for a total period of almost 24 hours. RUC interrogators, numbering as many as five at a time attempted to terrorise him into signing an incriminating statement. The most frightening time of all for Emmanuel was when, to quote his interrogators, 'his lights were out', by strangling him until he twice lost consciousness.

Emmanuel was forced to perform exhausting exercises and different forms of brutality were used against him including: slaps on the privates, straight finger jabs to the throat, heavy slaps on the head, being held in painful holds. An RUC man stuck his fingers in the back of Emmanuel's head, behind his ears, and raised him off the ground.

Despite all the assaults on him, which obviously caused him considerable pain and discomfort, Emmanuel's body was marked by only two small circular abrasions on his spine. Had he succumbed to his interrogators' pressure and signed a false confession his defence claim of ill-treatment would have received little substantiation from a medical examination.

Castlereagh
interrogation centre

164

IRA Volunteers at Casement Park Rally, Belfast, August, 1979

IRA unbeaten

Despite three years of torture in interrogation centres, Diplock courts and the H-Blocks, the IRA was undefeated and emerged at a massive rally for British withdrawal held at Casement Park on 12 August 1979. Armed Volunteers were greeted by cheering crowds.. Later that August the IRA's military capability was demonstrated when they ambushed and killed 18 British soldiers at Warrenpoint, Co. Down, and assassinated Lord Mountbatten. Sinn Féin Ard Rúnaí Dáithi Ó Conaill, a wanted man in the Six Counties, spoke at the Casement Park rally that marked a decade of struggle.

Many of you have lost your loved ones, thousands of you have passed through British jails and torture centres and all of us have known what it means to be a subject people in an occupied country. In common with previous generations, you too have known the vilification and misrepresentation which fighters for freedom the world over suffer until they are victorious.

And victorious we shall be. The seeds of victory were set in this city and in the city of Derry ten years ago when a risen people demonstrated clearly to themselves and to the world that fascist Stormont rule would no longer be tolerated.

And that desire was developed into deadly fighting action by units of the Irish Republican Army from Crossmaglen to the Sperrin Mountains. The enemy came to learn also that war is a two way traffic. When the IRA struck in England and further afield the English people came to realise that their government was central to the whole conflict in Ireland.

Rally for British withdrawal, Casement Park, Belfast, August, 1979

Response to Pope's visit

The world's media came to Ireland in September 1979 for the visit of Pope John Paul II. Sinn Féin responded with a detailed statement on the Irish situation which was delivered to an international press conference in Liberty Hall:

We note with satisfaction that Pope John Paul has reaffirmed that 'every human being has inalienable rights that must be respected' and that 'every human community' ethnic, historical, cultural or religious, has rights which must be respected...

Since 1976, the policies of both the British and Dublin governments has been to 'set aside the moral law in the interests of security and law and order', to quote Pope John Paul, by an intensification of repressive measures. These measures have produced barbaric prison conditions, deaths on hunger strike and the present obscenity of the H-Blocks of Long Kesh, now in its fourth year and which Cardinal O Fiach has described as 'one of the greatest obstacles to peace in our community'...

National H-Block Committee established

The establishment of the National Smash H-Block Committee at a conference in Belfast in October 1979 marked a stepping up of the campaign in support of the Republican prisoners. This resolution to establish the Committee was proposed by Sinn Féin Vice-President Gerry Adams:

(1) That this conference fully supports the protest for political status currently being waged by Republican prisoners of war and condemns the British Government for its barbaric treatment of prisoners, especially those incarcerated at Long Kesh and the women in Armagh Prison.

(2) This conference supports the proposal to elect a 17-person H-Block Committee to spearhead a national campaign of publicity and of militant protests in order to force the British Government to concede political prisoner status.

(3) This campaign headed by the Smash H-Block Committee should be oriented towards mobilising national support, particularly amongst the organised labour movement, community organisations and cultural organisations and also mobilising international support...

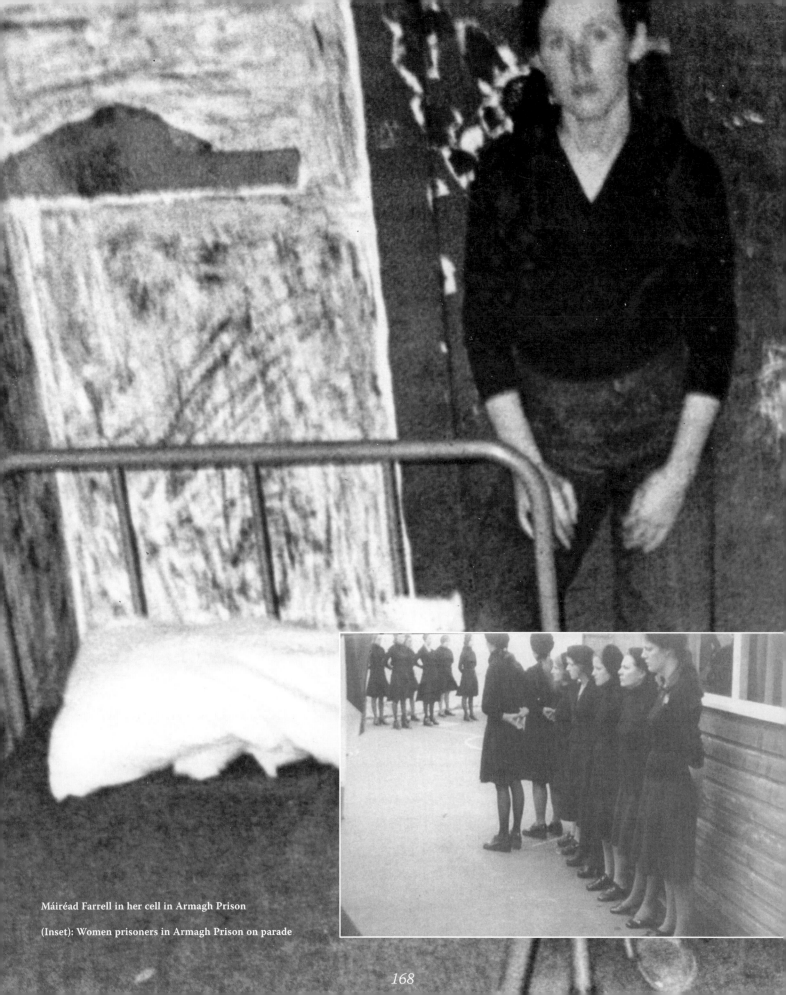

Máiréad Farrell in her cell in Armagh Prison

(Inset): Women prisoners in Armagh Prison on parade

Women prisoners attacked

Women Republican prisoners in Armagh Jail endured harsh conditions and in February 1980 were attacked by warders, signalling a serious deterioration in the regime. Anne Bateson described her ordeal:

On Thursday evening, 7th February, I was sitting in my cell when three male 'screws' burst in with riot gear. The three of them held me on the bed, then grabbed me by the arms and legs and dragged me out of the cell. At the same time they kept punching me. When they got me out to the wing, eight female screws took me from them. Helped by a male screw they carried me spread-eagled downstairs. The male screw had his hand on my throat the whole time and he kept pushing my head back. I thought I was going to choke.

I was carried into the guard room by the same screws — still spreadeagled and I was held in this position during the adjudication. My trousers and jumper were nearly off me at this stage but the Governor, Scott, told the screws to hold me in that position and not to let me down.

One of the screws said: "If you try to move it'll be your last time."

The male screws threw me into an empty cell. One of the male screws kicked me as I was lying on the floor.

Women in the New Ireland

Led by women such as Rita O'Hare and Martha McClelland, the women of Sinn Féin began to assert their rights within the Movement and within Irish society in 1980. This development, which coincided with the protest of women Republican prisoners in Armagh, was marked by the adoption at the 1980 Sinn Féin Ard Fheis of the landmark policy statement 'Women in the New Ireland'.

Women in Ireland face significant difficulties in their daily lives as a result of the long years of discrimination and injustice endured by them. James Connolly described the women of Ireland as 'the slaves of the slaves'.

This situation will not be resolved until the abysmal ignorance which surrounds it is wiped away. Men must realise that there is no innate threat to their position in the liberation of women, rather that they will be equal and this equality will help to liberate us all.

Sinn Féin says that in the New Ireland there will be no second-class citizens. Once this premise is accepted, it is obvious that close attention must be paid to the special repression directed against women and the resultant status of second class citizens.

This repression is not merely, nor even primarily, legislative. It is deep rooted, mainly inherited from Victorian England. It is interesting to note that in Celtic Ireland women had more equality with men than at any time since, and that divorce was allowed, and that the concept of illegitimacy was unheard of.

Sinn Féin activist Rita O'Hare with Máire Comerford who first got involved in Sinn Féin and Cumann na mBan in 1918.

Sinn Féin is not content just to recognise these problems. We are prepared to make these issues our own.

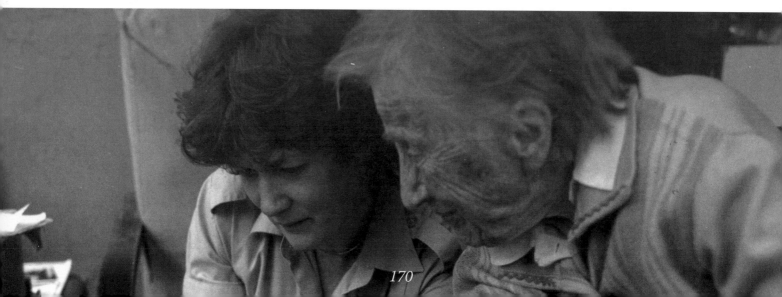

IRELAND
UNITED

BEHIND THE
HUNGER-STRIKE

Protest in support of the
Armagh Women in France,
1980.

Inset: An Phoblacht /
Republican News, 6 December
1980

FEMMES et MÈRES FEMMES et MÈRE
DE PRISONNIERS DE PRISONNIERS RÉ
IRLANDAIS
REPUBLICAINS NOUS NOUS DENONÇONS
DEMANDONS L'APPLICATI
DU
STATUT DE
PRISONNIERS POL

Second Hunger Strike announced

Statement of Blanket Men in the H-Blocks and women in Armagh, 5 February

We, the Republican political prisoners in the H-Blocks of Long Kesh and Armagh Prison, having waited patiently for seven weeks for evidence that the British Government was prepared to resolve the prison crisis and having given them every available opportunity to do so, declare our intention of hunger striking once more.

On December 18th and 19th 1980, the hunger strikes in the H-Blocks and Armagh Prison were ended. When this happened we were expecting that within a few days all protests could begin to be de-escalated and that the first hurdle, the blanket men receiving their own clothes, could be got over in the sequence described by [British direct ruler Humphrey] Atkins in his December 19th statement.

Obstacle after obstacle was put in our way but we felt morally bound to explore every avenue before giving in to exasperation and anger. The pettiness of the British administration was well demonstrated on January 23rd when the prison governor, acting under orders, refused a number of men their own clothes. These twenty men had taken part in successful wing shifts from dirty to clean cells and had begun slopping out, then washed, shaved and had their hair cut before applying for their own clothes.

It is a fact that ordinary prisoners in conforming blocks are generally wearing their own clothes unchallenged, and we were angered that the British were more intent upon humiliating us once again than on settling the prison crisis. Thus last Tuesday, 27th January, over ninety prisoners in the H-Blocks smashed up the cells as an expression of their anger.

However, in turn, the screws assaulted large numbers of men, moved them from clean cells into fouled cells, and overnight denied them blankets and mattresses, drinking water and access to the toilet...

We... have had enough of British deceit and broken promises. Hunger strikes to the death will begin, commencing from March 1st 1981, the fifth anniversary of the withdrawal of political status in the H-Blocks and Armagh Jail.

Diary of Bobby Sands from 1 March, Day 1 of the Hunger Strike

I am standing on the threshold of another trembling world. May God have mercy on my soul. My heart is very sore because I know that I have broken my poor mother's heart, and my home is struck with unbearable anxiety. But I have considered all the arguments and tried every means to avoid what has become the unavoidable: it has been forced upon me and my comrades by four and a half years of stark inhumanity.

I am a political prisoner. I am a political prisoner because I am a casualty of a perennial war that is being fought between the oppressed Irish people and an alien, oppressive, unwanted regime that refuses to withdraw from our land...

I believe I am but another of those wretched Irishmen born of a risen generation with a deeply rooted and unquenchable desire for freedom. I am dying not just to attempt to end the barbarity of H-Block, or to gain the rightful recognition of a political prisoner, but primarily because what is lost here is lost for the Republic and those wretched oppressed whom I am deeply proud to know as the "risen people".

Dialann Bobby Sands, Lá Fhéile Phádraig

Bhí mé ag smaoineamh inniu ar an chéalacán seo. Deireann daoine a lán faoin chorp ach ní chuireann muinín sa chorp ar bith. Measaim ceart go leor go bhfuil saghas troda. Ar dtús ní ghlacann leis an chorp an easpaidh bidh, is fulaingíonn sé an corp ar ais ceart go leor, ach deireadh an lae, téann achan rud ar ais chuig an phríomhrud, is é sin an mheabhair...

Mura bhfuil siad in inmhe an fonn saoirse a scriosadh, ní bheadh siad in inmhe tú féin a bhriseadh. Ní bhrisfidh siad mé mar tá an fonn saoirse, agus saoirse mhunitir na hEireann i mo chroí.

Tiocfaidh lá éigin nuair a bheidh an fonn saoirse seo le taispeáint ag daoine go léir na hEireann agus ansin tchífidh muid éirí na gealaí.

Bobby Sands elected MP for Fermanagh/South Tyrone

Bobby Sands was elected MP for Fermanagh and South Tyrone on 9 April. He secured 30,492 votes, as against 29,046 for Unionist Harry West. At the count in Enniskillen, Bobby's election agent, Owen Carron, spoke on his behalf:

A chairde, a dhaoine uaisle, ladies and gentlemen, on Bobby Sands's behalf I would like to claim victory. Bua do na príosúnaigh sna H-Blocks agus in Ard Mhacha.

The nationalist people spoke clearly and voted against Unionism and it is time for the British to do what they should have done long ago — get out.

Despite intimidation from the so-called security forces, the voters of Fermanagh and South Tyrone stood by the prisoners and told Mrs. Thatcher today, that we, on behalf of the Irish people, will not accept the situation in the H-Blocks and we demand an immediate end to that intolerable situation.

Death of Bobby Sands

Bobby Sands died on 5 May 1981. His funeral was one of the largest ever seen in Ireland. Among the many tributes paid to him was this from Danny Morrison, then Editor of An Phoblacht/Republican News:

I remember well the first time I met Bobby Sands. It was in May 1976... He walked into the offices of the Belfast Republican Press Centre, which I had just recently joined, and was looking for duplicating paper and stencils so that he could get leaflets out in the Twinbrook estate for a tenants' association and to kindle interest in the idea of a youth club for the area. His short hair was fair to ginger and he had the fresh face of youth and made a sharp contrast with the next time I was to meet him in January 1980 when his hair was long, greasy and matted, his face sporting an eight-inch beard.

But the young man that stood behind our counter in 1976 was every bit as intense and dedicated as the blanket leader of 1981. Fellow press centre worker Tom Hartley and I spotted him right away and attempted to lure him into the centre, which was then in its comparative infancy; but he wanted to work in his own area which was, as we suspected, his base as an IRA freedom fighter...

In the H-Blocks the Brits saw the opportunity to defeat the IRA by criminalising the Irish freedom fighters. But the blanket men, perhaps even more than those on the outside, appreciated before anyone else the grave repercussions of a defeat and so they fought. They fought with a determination, courage and political dedication which came to be symbolised in Bobby and the other hunger strikers.

Bobby Sands was a truly unique person whose loss is great and immeasurable. He had so much life in him but it was repressed and murdered by the English hands of imperial Britain which still scars our land.

My dear friend and comrade, although it has happened I still cannot believe it. I would have liked to have said goodbye and shook that sure strong hand once more, but that was denied us. You are at peace now, out of the hell blocks that murdered you, out of the clutches of the screws and British rule, like the lark free and at peace. Now we need your prayers, your courage and your determination, that beautiful unvanquished spirit that brought you through those tribulations. Watch over us.

Funeral of Bobby Sands

179

Martin McGuinness at the graveside of Francis Hughes

Some may ask, 'What do you mean he died for Irish freedom? Was it not because of prison clothes and prison work?' What I mean is this. The British Government decided prior to March 1st 1976 that they were unable to defeat the IRA in their overall war effort; that they needed a psychological victory over republicans and that a battle must be fought which they must be sure of winning. So armed with their tanks and guns, torture centres, H-Blocks and a multi-million-pound propaganda machine they set about a criminalisation policy against republican prisoners of war, who were armed with nothing but their moral courage to resist...

His body lies here beside us. But he lives in the little streets of Belfast, he lives in the Bogside, he lives in East Tyrone, he lives in Crossmaglen. He will always live in the hearts and minds of unconquerable Irish republicans in these places.

They could not break him.

They will not break us.

Joe McDonnell's family grieve at his funeral

Plastic bullet deaths

Among several young people killed by plastic bullets fired by the RUC and British Army in 1981 was 12-year-old Carol-Ann Kelly. An Phoblacht/Republican News *reported:*

After the death of young Julie Livingstone a fortnight ago and the injuring of several other school children by plastic bullets, Brit and RUC patrols have injured a further five children, one of them shot twice in the back with live rounds. One of the most outrageous shootings was the killing of 12-year-old Carol-Ann Kelly, from the Twinbrook area of West Belfast, who was struck on the head and fatally wounded by a plastic bullet fired at a range of several yards.

Carol-Ann had been coming out of a shop in Aspen Park with two friends at 8.30pm on Tuesday, May 19th. She was carrying a carton of milk which her mother had sent her to the shops to fetch. There were few people on the street when five British Army jeeps entered the area... As they came to the spot where Carol-Ann was standing, the Brits in the first two jeeps opened fire with plastic bullets and without any warning. Carol-Ann's two friends dived for cover but Carol-Ann was not so fortunate.

She was struck in the head by one of the bullets and knocked unconscious. When local people reached her she was bleeding profusely from the wound. Neighbours called an ambulance, which arrived after fifteen minutes, the delay being caused by the British Army who initially sent it away from the scene. Carol-Ann was taken to hospital where she was operated on, and survived on a life support machine until her death on Friday May 22nd.

Dublin establishment spurns prisoner TDs

The General Election in the 26 Counties in June 1981 saw victory for hunger striker Kieran Doherty in Cavan/Monaghan and H-Block prisoner Paddy Agnew in Louth. Nine prisoners in all contested the election. Charles Haughey, who had been Taoiseach since 1979, was replaced by a Fine Gael/Labour Coalition led by Garret FitzGerald. Like Haughey, he refused to support the prisoners' five demands. His fellow TD, Kieran Doherty, died on 2 August. At Kieran Doherty's funeral, his election agent, future Sinn Féin TD Caoimhghín Ó Caoláin, denounced the Dublin establishment:

Their gamesmanship for petty political scores has been a major factor in the continuing deaths in Long Kesh. The people of Cavan/Monaghan hold the present Coalition government directly

responsible, through firstly their inactivity, and afterwards their open support for pressure to be placed on the hunger strikers through their families.

H-Block protest at Leinster House after the election of Kieran Doherty TD

Garret FitzGerald never liked Republicans and we who know his ilk identify him only with the pro-British establishment that has eaten its way back into control over all aspects of Free State life. The elected colleagues of Kieran Doherty are not here today.

RTÉ censors prisoners' MP

Owen Carron was elected MP for Fermanagh/South Tyrone with an increased vote in the by-election that followed the death of Bobby Sands. The Thatcher government had passed legislation that prevented prisoners from contesting elections and Carron stood as an anti-H-Block/Armagh candidate. RTÉ invoked Section 31 of the Broadcasting Act, the political censorship provision in the 26 Counties, to ban Carron as An Phoblacht/Republican News *reported:*

The RTÉ television news programmes began, on Friday evening, August 21st, with the returning officer for Fermanagh and South Tyrone reading out the votes gained by each candidate in the previous day's by-election. As Owen Carron moved to the microphones to make his acceptance speech he was abruptly cut off and thus ended the total news coverage of an indisputably significant event in Ireland, for those in the single-channel areas of the 26 Counties. The one million or more watchers of BBC and ITV in the Free State could, of course, hear what the elected representative of the 31,278 of their fellow countrymen had to say, both in his speech and in the long interviews which followed.

The Hunger Strike ends

On 3 October, the prisoners in the H-Blocks announced the end of the Hunger Strike. They explained their reasons in a statement that marked the end of one of the most colossal struggles in Irish history:

Why we ended the Hunger Strike

We the protesting republican prisoners in the H-Blocks, being faced with the reality of sustained family intervention, are forced by this circumstance, over which we have little control at the moment, to end the hunger strike...

There were several reasons given by our comrades for going on hunger strike. One was because we had no choice and no other means of securing a principled solution to the four-year protest. Another, and of fundamental importance, was to advance the Irish people's right to liberty. We believe that the age-old struggle for Irish self-determination and freedom has been immeasurably advanced by this hunger strike and therefore we claim a massive political victory. The hunger strikers by their sacrifice have politicised a very substantial section of the Irish nation and exposed the shallow, unprincipled nature of the Irish partitionist bloc.

Our comrades have lit with their very lives an eternal beacon which will inspire this nation and people to rise and crush oppression forever and this nation can be proud that it produced such a quality of manhood.

We pay a special tribute to the families of our dead comrades. You have suffered greatly and with immense dignity. Your loved ones, our comrades and friends, were and would be very proud of you for standing by them. No tribute is too great.

Also, we give a special mention to those families who could not bear to watch their loved ones die in pain and agony. We prisoners understand the pressure you were under and stand by you.

We thank the National H-Block/Armagh Committee, the H-Block movement, the nationalist people of Ireland, and all those who championed our cause abroad...

Lastly we reaffirm our commitment to the achievement of the five demands by whatever means we believe necessary and expedient. We rule nothing out. Under no circumstances are we going to devalue the memory of our dead comrades by submitting ourselves to a dehumanising and degrading regime.

Bobby Sands

Kevin Lynch

Francis Hughes

Joe McDonnell

Kieran Doherty

Martin Hurson

Raymond McCreesh

Thomas McElwee

Patsy O'Hara

Micky Devine

Electoral strategy under way

The 1981 Sinn Féin Ard Fheis came in the wake of the Hunger Strikes and was inspired by the sacrifices of the ten young Republicans in the H-Blocks. It also saw key debates on the policy and strategy of the party. Federalism — the concept of four provincial parliaments in a new Ireland — was dropped. More significantly, the way was opened for Sinn Féin to contest and take seats in local government elections in the Six Counties which had previously been boycotted. The Ard Fheis gave authority to the Ard Chomhairle to decide on involvement in Leinster House, Stormont and Westminster elections on an abstentionist basis. The most remembered — and misquoted — contribution of the Ard Fheis was that of Director of Publicity Danny Morrison.

Ballot paper and Armalite

Who here really believes we can win the war through the ballot box? But will anyone here object if, with a ballot paper in this hand, and an Armalite in this hand, we take power in Ireland?

Leinster House election contested on abstentionist basis

Sinn Féin stood seven candidates in the February 1982 Leinster House elections. Two were Republican prisoners — Seamus McElwaine in Cavan/Monaghan, who was killed on active service with the IRA in 1986, and Joe O'Connell, one of the Balcombe Street men serving a life sentence in England. It was the first time for 20 years that Sinn Féin contested a Leinster House election. With just under 17,000 votes between them, the candidates picked up around half of the H-Block votes of the previous June.

Adams elected President of Sinn Féin

Ruairi O Brádaigh stepped down as President of Sinn Féin and Gerry Adams was elected unopposed at the 1983 Ard Fheis. In a wide-ranging address he addressed armed struggle and the future role of Sinn Féin:

It became clear to many that it was no longer sufficient to be passive supporters of the IRA and more and more people realised that, insofar as the IRA had established a military alternative to the British war machine, that they, as republicans, had a duty and a responsibility to establish alternatives to all the other facets of British involvement on this island. Sinn Féin with its increased and growing membership, began to develop attitudes towards and alternatives to the social, political, economic and cultural aspects of British rule in the Six Counties. The results of this work are clearly evident in our dramatic electoral successes over the past year and in the high morale of our supporters...

In defending and supporting the right of the Irish people to engage in armed struggle, it is important for those so engaged to be aware of the constant need to continuously examine their tactics and strategies. Revolutionary force — and this excludes sectarian violence — must be controlled and disciplined so that it is clearly seen as a symbol for the people's resistance...

Gerry Adams and Alex
Maskey on the election trail

Labour and Fine Gael boycott Sinn Féin

In 1984, the Fine Gael/Labour Coalition began refusing to meet local government delegations that included Sinn Féin councillors. Among those who withdrew from meetings so that other members of the delegation could meet ministers was Donegal County Councillor Eddie Fullerton. After Labour Environment Minister Liam Kavanagh refused to meet Eddie at Leinster House, Eddie spoke to the press:

I think this is a diabolical travesty of democracy. This is the first time in my five years on the Council that I've ever come across this. Democracy has been turned around on its head.

I decided that if I stayed, then Kavanagh would have had his excuse to do nothing for Buncrana and, rather than let him worm his way out by scoring political points, I left.

If he was going to deny me the right to represent the people who voted for me, I had no intention of giving him the excuse to deny their needs.

Donegal Sinn Féin County Councillor, Eddie Fullerton, at Leinster House in 1984

RUC attacks on Republican funerals

Republican funerals attacked by the RUC

Between December 1983 and May 1987, over 25 Republican funerals were attacked by the RUC. Like the hijacking of the body of Proinsias Stagg' in 1974 by the Dublin Government, this was a British strategy to suppress public displays of support for the IRA. At the funeral of IRA Volunteer Larry Marley in Ardoyne in April 1987 this strategy culminated in the delay of the funeral for days as hundreds of RUC and British soldiers besieged the Marley home. But the Republican funeral went ahead and Martin McGuinness spoke at the graveside:

This funeral has seen a further intensification of RUC attacks on the rights of bereaved Republican families and their friends. Even in death there is no peace. On Monday, they set out to break, degrade and humiliate Larry's family and us, their friends, but Kate Marley and her young children broke the RUC. We salute their courage.

The Bishops have no difficulty over Free State Army firing parties and guards of honour in chapel yards the length and breadth of Ireland. Only yesterday a member of the British Army who was killed in Divis Flats was buried in England. He was a Catholic. His Union Jack-draped coffin was carried out of the Catholic church by six uniformed members of the British Army, taken to an adjoining graveyard, and a volley of shots fired by his colleagues. It's not the guns they object to but who holds them....

Loughgall

At Loughgall, County Armagh, in May 1987 the British Army ambushed and killed eight IRA Volunteers and a civilian. It was the largest loss of life suffered by the IRA in a single incident since the Civil War. Gerry Adams spoke at the funeral of Volunteer Tony Gormle:

Loughgall will not end the republican struggle. I don't say that because I am staunch or defiant. I say that as a fact of reality. This is Ireland. Mise Eire. Sine mé ná an chailleach Bhéara. Mór mo ghlóir do rug Cú Chulainn cróga. This is Ireland. The British Government has no right to be in this country. It has no right to partition this country. It has no right to visit this injustice on us...

You don't have to join the IRA as he did, you don't have to join Sinn Féin, you don't have to go to prison, but you do have to stand up and speak out against injustice... Loughgall was wrong. What caused Loughgall is wrong. War is wrong. But the conditions in this country which cause war are evil.

We will remember Tony Gormley and we will remember Loughgall. And Margaret Thatcher and Tom King and all the other rich and powerful people will be sorry, in their time, that Loughgall happened. And Tony Gormley is dead, but in a new, peaceful Ireland, Tony Gormley will never die.

The scene in the aftermath of the Loughgall ambush

Inset: The IRA fires a volley of shots at the funeral of Volunteer Jim Lynagh

Enniskillen

Eleven people were killed when an IRA bomb exploded during a Remembrance Day ceremony in Enniskillen, Co. Fermanagh, in November 1987. It was one of the worst tragedies of the conflict. In an interview in An Phoblacht, *Gerry Adams addressed the responsibility of Republicans:*

Every IRA Volunteer must realise that he or she has the capacity to advance or retard the national struggle. The British crown forces will exploit IRA operational mistakes in a ruthless manner. They have no concern for the civilian population. Concern for the civilian population must be a key factor in the IRA's deliberations. I deeply regret that Enniskillen happened and my sympathy is with the relatives of the dead and injured. Their dignity in mourning was very moving and their forgiveness, and particularly the words of Mr. [Gordon] Wilson, had a deep effect on me and I am sure on other Republicans, much more so that the nauseating wave of condemnations that were heaped on us by a wide range of self-righteous political and religious leaders.

March '88 — month of tragedy

In March 1988, in Gibraltar, undercover British soldiers shot dead three unarmed IRA Volunteers - Mairéad Farrell, Dan McCann and Seán Savage. Thousands turned out for their funerals which began with the return of their bodies to Dublin and their journey to Belfast. In Milltown Cemetery the funeral was attacked with gun and grenades by a loyalist who killed three people and injured many more. At the funeral of one of the victims, IRA Volunteer Caoimhín Mac Brádaigh, two armed and plainclothed British soldiers drove into the cortege. After they opened fire they were seized by the crowd before being executed by the IRA. Following these events the nationalist people of West Belfast were demonised in the establishment media. Part of the response to that demonisation was the growth of Féile an Phobail, the West Belfast Festival, which celebrates the energy, heritage, culture and politics of the area.

The scene of the shootings in Gibraltar where Mairead Farrell, Dan McCann and Seán Savage were killed by undercover British soldiers.

Inset: The funeral of the three Volunteers at Dublin Airport

Mourners under attack in Milltown Cemetery at the funeral of the Gibraltar Volunteers.

Sinn Féin/SDLP talks

Talks between Sinn Féin and the SDLP during 1988 were an important prelude to the peace process. While they did not reach agreement on a common approach, a foundation had been laid for future dialogue.

Sinn Féin statement on conclusion of talks with the SDLP

At the beginning of this year Sinn Féin and the SDLP received a written invitation from a third party to engage in a political dialogue aimed at investigating the possibility of developing "an overall political strategy to establish justice and peace in Ireland". Any suggestion that the talks had any other purpose is untrue.

During this dialogue several position papers and analyses were exchanged.
From the outset, our proposals were based on our overall view that justice and peace can best be established when the Irish nation can exercise its right to national self-determination and the conflict over British interference in Irish sovereignty is resolved.

Sinn Féin believes that any strategy which seeks to establish national self-determination must have as its objectives:

- To persuade the British Government to change its current policy of partition to one of ending the Union and handing sovereignty to an all-Ireland government whose selection would be a democratic matter for the Irish nation,
- To persuade the unionists that their future lies in this context and to persuade the British Government that it has a responsibility to so influence unionist attitudes.

The method of achieving these objectives should include:

- The securing of maximum political unity in Ireland based on these objectives,
- The launching of a concerted political campaign internationally, using Dublin government diplomatic resources to win international support for Irish demands,
- The mobilising of support in Britain itself which would create conditions in which the right to Irish self-determination can be exercised.

During this campaign a debate, aimed at leading to dialogue, must be initiated with northern Protestants and northern Protestant opinion on the democratic principle of national self-determination.

They must be assured by our full commitment to their civil and religious rights and be persuaded of the need for their participation in building an Irish society based on equality and national reconciliation.

There is also a need to establish a democratic structure by which the above can be agreed upon, implemented and overseen, or, failing this, to encourage informal agreement to implement the above.

Finally, Sinn Féin believes that there must be concerted political action, nationally and internationally, to defend democratic rights and to defend and improve the social and economic rights and conditions of the population of the Six Counties and that transgressions of these rights must be exposed.

The Thatcher government imposed a broadcasting ban on Sinn Féin in 1988

British broadcasting ban

Sinn Féin had been barred from radio and TV in the 26 Counties since 1971. In October 1988, the British Government introduced a similar ban which they kept in place until 1994. Gerry Adams responded:

This draconian measure is not an attack on the IRA or the ability of the IRA to operate. It is a direct attack on Sinn Féin because Sinn Féin's views are unacceptable to the British Government and because we reject British claims of sovereignty over the Six Counties and articulate the demand for national self-determination.

Cllr. Alex Maskey with an example of the thousands of RUC files on nationalists passed on to loyalist death squads

Mr. John Davey

Collusion claims lives of leading nationalists

In 1989, the campaign of assassination of leading nationalists and republicans, carried out by loyalists with the active assistance of British forces, was at its height. At the same time, ordinary Catholics continued to be murdered simply because of their religion or perceived political affiliation. One week in February told the story as reported in An Phoblacht. *Collusion became a key issue for Sinn Féin in the 1990s.*

John Davey, a veteran republican of 30 years standing and an elected representative of his people on Magherafelt District Council, was shot dead on Tuesday night, February 14th. He was the third nationalist to die in a week in a renewed onslaught of sectarian murders. The killing of the Sinn Féin councillor came just two days after the death of leading civil rights lawyer Pat Finucane and the slaying the previous Thursday of Belfast Catholic Tony Fusco. Each killing in its own way showed a different aspect of loyalist terror tactics which have the collusion of the British military in the North. Together they represent the systematic intimidation of an entire community — a purpose completely at one with British military strategy in the Six Counties which seeks to keep nationalists under a constant state of siege.

Murdered Civil Rights lawyer Pat Finucane (right) with the late Pat McGeown, former H-Block Hunger Striker and Sinn Féin Ard Chomhairle member

Martin McGuinness helps local communities along the
border re-open roads closed by the British Government.

Ireland's 'Berlin Wall'

1989 saw local communities in the Border Counties, in conjunction with Sinn Féin, commencing a campaign of reopening the scores of cross-Border roads forcibly closed by the British Army. In the week in November 1989, when the Berlin Wall was torn down, communities gathered along the Border to reopen the roads.. They were met by heavily armed RUC and British soldiers. Monaghan Sinn Féin County Councillor Pat Treanor commented:

The actions of the British Army and RUC in crushing this community effort to re-establish cross-border links contrasts greatly with what is going on elsewhere in Europe at this time. That blinkered clergyman Bishop Cahal Daly has been asked to speak out against this injustice. His silence, although whole communities have been rent asunder in this way, exposes his hypocrisy and that of his 'Peace Train' cronies for all to see.

Brooke challenged on peace

British Secretary of State in the Six Counties Peter Brooke gave an interview at the end of 1989 in which he admitted that the IRA would not be militarily defeated. In his 1990 Presidential Address at the Sinn Féin Ard Fheis, Gerry Adams responded:

Serious observers of the conflict in Ireland, including the British Government, know that talks with Sinn Féin are inevitable. What then, is the justification for refusing to talk now? The failure to do what they know they will do in the future is prolonging the conflict and perpetuating the suffering for both the Irish and the British people...

Sinn Féin is ready at any time to discuss the conditions in which peace and justice can be established. We are actively endeavouring to create such conditions...

It was the ongoing failure of the British and their unionist allies to subvert a popular struggle of resistance to British rule in the Six Counties, allied to the emergence of Sinn Féin as an electoral force in the wake of the heroic hunger strikes and the IRA's continued ability and capacity to strike telling blows against the colonial regime, which led to the Hillsborough Treaty. Its aim was to defeat us. It has failed to do so.

Nelson Mandela calls for Irish peace talks

In July 1990, South African leader Nelson Mandela, who had been released in February after 25 years as a political prisoner, visited Ireland and called for peace talks, much to the displeasure of the Irish and British establishment. Mr Mandela said:

What we would like to see is that the British Government and the IRA should adopt precisely the line we have taken with regard to our internal situation. There is nothing better than opponents sitting down to resolve our problems in a peaceful manner...

What I am concerned with is a peaceful solution and, as you know, the British Government has involved itself in negotiations before when parties were fighting. There are precedents. During the continuation of the conflict, the British Government, without insisting that any side should lay down arms, got involved and was able to... induce all parties to conclude peace.

Martin McGuinness and Gerry Adams meet Nelson Mandela in Dublin

This was the position in Rhodesia... It is a principle that is applied all over the world, in all situations...

Political extradition

Protests at the extradition of Dessie Ellis outside the Four Courts, Dublin

Throughout the 1980s, court judgements and legislation, culminating in the 1987 Extradition Act, eroded the protection of citizens from extradition to the Six Counties and Britain for political offences. Extradition became a major political campaign for Sinn Féin. In November 1990, Dublin Republican Dessie Ellis embarked on a hunger strike against his extradition to England to face conspiracy charges. Days prior to his handover to Britain, thousands demonstrated and his sister Martha addressed them at the GPO:

Charles Haughey is trying along with the rest of his government to have my brother extradited to face conspiracy charges. My brother has said all along if the British have evidence against him then let them present it in an Irish court. Dessie is only asking for what Charles Haughey got 20 years ago. Yet Haughey, Burke, Collins, Lenihan and Co. have refused that to Dessie.

Last week the Birmingham Six said they have lost all confidence in the Irish Government, which had done little for them. We have no confidence in this government to do the right thing, the just thing, the humane thing.

Revisionists answered

Thousands of people from all over Ireland gathered in Dublin to mark the 75th anniversary of the 1916 Rising in 1991. There was no official State marking of the occasion as establishment politicians and anti-nationalist historians sought to play down its significance. But Republican Ireland came together under the banner of the Reclaim the Spirit of 1916 organisation. Artist Robert Ballagh addressed the ceremony:

It has been a revealing experience to witness the serried ranks of the southern establishment squirm in the face of their own history... However, seduced by their powerful position and through isolation from the real people, they made a major miscalculation. Viewing Ireland from their ivory towers and writing and commenting loftily in their newspaper columns and on radio and television, they presumed that when they read and heard what they themselves wrote and said, that that somehow represented public opinion. Oh, how the mighty have fallen.

Out of their own mouths in opinion polls and discussion programmes they have been proved wrong. The Irish people wanted to celebrate the 75th anniversary of 1916 and they have been showing that over the past few weeks all over the country and not least here today.

Collusion targets Sinn Féin members

1991 saw a further escalation in the campaign of assassination of Sinn Féin members. In the run-up to the local elections in the 26 Counties in May, Donegal County Councillor Eddie Fullerton was murdered in his home in Buncrana. In August, Sinn Féin members Pádraig O Seanacháin of County Tyrone and Tommy Donaghy of County Derry were murdered. Then, in September, Magherafelt Councillor Bernard O'Hagan was slain, the third Sinn Féin Councillor to be killed within 18 months. Eddie Fullerton's New Year's resolution for 1991 was found among his papers.

Eddie Fullerton's New Year's resolution

My sincere and most desirable wish for the year 1991 would be the withdrawal of the British Army of occupation, the release of all political prisoners and freedom, justice and peace established throughout the whole of Ireland. Peace in the world without war. An Ireland with full employment, no emigration, where all the Irish people could live in a free and just society in complete harmony, prosperity and peace.

Cllr. Bernard O'Hagan

Black flag protest after the RUC murder of John Downes, when the RUC attacked a Sinn Féin rally in West Belfast, August, 1984

Gerry Adams, Albert Reynolds
and John Hume at Dublin
Government Buildings in the wake
of the first IRA cessation,
September 1994

Building peace and freedom

1992-2005

Bid to ban Ard Fheis fails
Sheena Campbell
Year of tragedy and hope
Hume/Adams initiatives
British Government lies exposed
Section 31 ban lifted
IRA declares cessation
500 days and no talks
British bin Mitchell — IRA ends cessation
Two MPs and one TD
Good Friday Agreement
Executive established
Holy Cross
All-Ireland breakthrough for Sinn Féin
Joe Cahill — 1920-2004
2 MEPs, 252 Councillors, 24 MLAs, 5 TDs, 5 MPs

Bid to ban Ard Fheis fails

In November 1991, in a move led by the Labour Party's Ruairi Quinn, Dublin City Council voted to deny Sinn Féin the use of the Mansion House for its Ard Fheis. The Ard Fheis was hosted in Ballyfermot Community Centre in February 1992 and it endorsed the landmark document 'Towards a Lasting Peace in Ireland', a key stage in the development of the peace process, summarised here.

Towards a Lasting Peace in Ireland

1. Peace requires the conditions of democracy, freedom and justice to eradicate the causes of war.

2. The Irish people have the same historical right to sovereignty and nationhood which is recognized by international law. Partition contravenes these laws and frustrates national democracy and national reconciliation.

3. British rule in Ireland has no democratic legitimacy and has rested on division and coercion. They should recognize the failure of partition.

4. The Dublin Government should assume its responsibility in relation to reunification either in co-operation with Britain or, if necessary, independently.

5. The unionist minority have nothing to fear from a united Ireland. Removing the veto will open up the possibility for constructive dialogue.

6. Irish republicans are committed to playing a constructive role in building national democracy when the British Government finally adopts a policy of withdrawal from Ireland.

7. The partition of Ireland and the British claim to jurisdiction over the Six Counties is a European issue.

8. The United Nations has the authority and mandate to monitor a decolonisation process in Ireland. As an interim measure, Sinn Féin would propose that the United Nations monitors partition and Britain's role within it.

Sinn Féin protest confronted by Gardaí

Sheena Campbell

The murder of Sheena Campbell, law student, leading Sinn Féin activist and electoral strategist, in Belfast's York Hotel on 16 October 1992, marked a further escalation in the campaign against the party. Jim McAllister spoke prophetic words at her funeral:

You can censor us, call us thugs and murderers, call us fanatics and lunatics, you can refuse to speak to us, extradite us, ban us, torture us and kill us, but there will always be enough of us to ensure that one day you will talk to us...

You are the shameful ones who sit cosily with the British who destroy our homes, our lands and our lives. You are the shameful ones, you cardinals and moderators who preach love but practice discrimination and the politics of exclusion while you sit with the masters of people like Brian Nelson.

You are the shameful ones, you Leinster House gombeens and your media puppets in RTÉ who laud the praises of those who maintain partition in Ireland; who say that emigration is the solution to unemployment and that the freedom struggle ended 70 years ago...

Sinn Féin Councillors protest after the murder of Sheena Campbell.

(inset): Sinn Féin Ard Rúnaí Lucilita Bhreatnach at the funeral of Sheena Campbell

Year of tragedy and hope

1993 was one of the most tragic years of the conflict. It was also a year of hope as efforts escalated to create a real peace process. Sectarian assassinations of nationalist civilians — including two members of Sinn Féin — continued at an appalling rate. Two children were killed in an IRA bombing in the English town of Warrington in March. In October, seven civilians were killed by the UDA in a bar in Greysteel, County Derry. This followed the death of nine civilians and an IRA Volunteer in the IRA bombing of a Shankill Road shop, aimed at a UDA meeting. While Republicans were rightly criticised, the victims of sectarian loyalist attacks and collusion were largely ignored, especially by establishment politicians and media in the 26 Counties.. An Phoblacht *counted the cost of collusion.*

Toll of collusion

In January 1988, the South African arms shipment arrived in the Six Counties with British intelligence approval and support. It contained:

- 200 AK47 rifles
- 90 Browning 9mm pistols
- 500 fragmentation grenades
- 3,000 rounds of ammunition
- 12 RPG rocket launchers.

From January 1988 until [21] October 1993:

- A total of 146 sectarian killings have been carried out by loyalists
- 67 of those are known to have been killed by the weapons contained in the South African shipment
- In all probability, the remaining 79 killings were carried out with South African weapons
- From 1990 until now, loyalist death squads have killed more people in the North than anyone else
- The RUC has abandoned its former policy and now refuses to disclose forensic details on the weapons used by loyalists
- The loyalists have thousands of RUC/RIR-supplied files in their possession
- The RUC/RIR/British Army have files on almost every nationalist household.

Hume-Adams initiative

The key dialogue that began a real peace initiative was that between Gerry Adams and John Hume. In June 1993, they issued a joint statement:

A meeting between us held on Saturday, 10 April, in our capacities as party leaders of the SDLP and Sinn Féin, has given rise to media coverage, some of which was ill-informed or purely speculative.

We are not acting as intermediaries. As leaders of our respective parties, we accept that the most pressing issue facing the people of Ireland and Britain today is the question of lasting peace and how it can best be achieved.

Everyone has a solemn duty to change the political climate away from conflict and towards a process of national reconciliation which sees the peaceful accommodation of the differences between the people of Britain and Ireland and the Irish people themselves.

In striving for that end we accept that an internal settlement is not a solution because it obviously does not deal with all the relationships at the heart of the problem.

We accept that the Irish people as a whole have a right to national self-determination. This is a view shared by a majority of the people of this island, though not by all its people.

The exercise of self-determination is a matter for agreement between the people of Ireland. It is the search for that agreement and the means of achieving it on which we will be concentrating...

British Government lies exposed

Having repeatedly denied that they had maintained contacts with Sinn Féin, the British Government was forced into an embarrassing climb-down in November 1993. Secretary of State Patrick Mayhew published a censored selection of statements and documents exchanged between the British Government and Sinn Féin. The party quickly responded, publishing the full correspondence and exposing the duplicity of a British government that still claimed that there could be no dialogue with Sinn Féin before an IRA ceasefire:

A line of communication has existed between Sinn Féin and the British Government for over 20 years. It has not been in constant use. It has been used in an intensive way during such periods as the bilateral truce of 1974-75 and the Long Kesh Hunger Strikes of 1980 and 1981.

The British Government reactivated it in the middle of 1990. This led to a period of protracted contact and dialogue between Sinn Féin and the British Government.

At all times Sinn Féin has endeavoured to avoid the disclosure of this line of communication even when such revelations would have been to our advantage or to the disadvantage of the British Government.

The British Government has shown no such integrity. In the course of the recent protracted contact and dialogue, Sinn Féin made a number of complaints to the British Government about leaks to the media. These leaks are documented both in the Sinn Féin record and in the British Government version.

In the early part of 1993, the British Government proposed a series of meetings with Sinn Féin, arguing that an intensive round of such meetings would result in Irish Republicans being convinced that armed struggle was no longer necessary. They requested a two to three week undeclared suspension of operations by the Irish Republican Army to facilitate this. Sinn Féin sought and gained such a commitment from the IRA. This was communicated to the British Government on 10 May 1993.

There was no positive response to this and after some time it became quite clear that the British Government was attempting to disguise its rejection of the substantial response by the IRA to its request.

Simultaneously, the volume of leaks and rumours about talks between Sinn Féin and the British Government noticeably increased.

The leaks led to the breaking of the story on 8 November 1993, by Belfast journalist, Eamon Mallie. There were immediate British Government denials. One of these leaks was from DUP MP Willie McCrea. According to Mr. McCrea he was given a copy of a British communiqué by a senior civil servant in the Northern Ireland Office...

Section 31 ban lifted

Larry O'Toole, whose court case against Section 31 censorship paved the way for the ban to be lifted.

21 years on from the sacking of the RTÉ Authority and the tightening of the radio and TV ban on Sinn Féin in the 26 Counties, the ban was finally lifted by the Irish Government in January 1994. Fine Gael leader John Bruton said its removal would hinder the search for peace. Sinn Féin's response was given by Larry O'Toole, the trade unionist who successfully challenged RTÉ's interpretation of Section 31 in the courts:

21 years of Section 31 censorship has exacerbated the problem and prevented real dialogue. It has denied people's right to information. It has denied a voice to Sinn Féin voters and has led to a situation where people in the South don't know what is happening north of the border.

Ending Section 31 at this time would be a valuable contribution to the search for a just peace. Where is the logic in arguing that a full and open debate would hinder the search for peace?

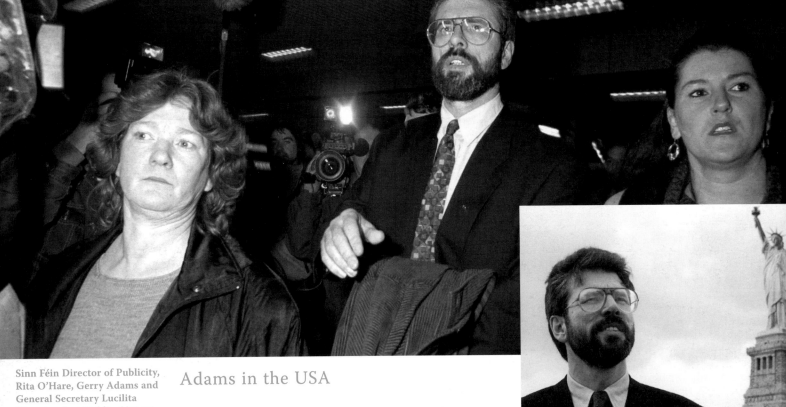

Sinn Féin Director of Publicity, Rita O'Hare, Gerry Adams and General Secretary Lucilita Bhreatnach at Dublin Airport prior to his first visit to the USA, 1994

Adams in the USA

The censorship of Sinn Féin by denying visas to their spokespersons to visit the USA was ended by President Bill Clinton in February 1994 when Gerry Adams was granted a visa to visit New York. He spoke there for the first time:

I thank all those who helped to secure a visa for me to attend this conference, and the many Irish-Americans and supporters of free speech who have tirelessly campaigned against visa denial. I wish to extend greetings also to the many people here in the USA who have worked consistently for the cause of freedom, justice and peace in Ireland.

IRA declares cessation

On 31 August 1994, the IRA announced a complete cessation of military operations.

At this historic crossroads, the leadership of Óglaigh na hÉireann salutes and commends our Volunteers, other activists, our supporters and the political prisoners who have sustained this struggle for the past 25 years. Your courage, determination and sacrifices have demonstrated that the spirit of freedom and the desire for peace based on a just and lasting settlement cannot be crushed. We remember all those who have died for Irish freedom and we reiterate our commitment to our republican objectives...

A solution will only be found as a result of inclusive negotiations. Others, not least the British Government, have a duty to face up to their responsibilities. It is our desire to significantly contribute to the creation of a climate which will encourage this. We urge everyone to approach this new situation with energy, determination and patience....

Gerry Adams, Marie
Moore and Martin
McGuinness at a West
Belfast rally after the IRA
cessation was announced

British bin Mitchell — IRA ends cessation

The International Body headed by George Mitchell recommended that all-party talks should go ahead. In January 1996, its report was binned by John Major who conceded to the Unionist demand for elections before talks. On 9 February, the IRA ended its cessation when it bombed Canary Wharf in London and explained its motivation:

The cessation presented an historic challenge for everyone and the Irish Republican Army commends the leadership of nationalist Ireland at home and abroad. They rose to the challenge. The British Prime Minister did not. Instead of embracing the peace process, the British Government acted in bad faith, with Mr. Major and the unionist leaders squandering this opportunity to resolve the conflict... The blame for the failure thus far of the Irish peace process lies squarely with John Major and his government.

116,000 voters locked out

Elections were held to a forum in the Six Counties in May 1996. Sinn Féin secured over 116,000 votes, 42% of the nationalist electorate, but was locked out of the talks at Stormont the following month. Martin McGuinness spoke at the gates of Stormont:

We have cleared in the last number of years every single precondition placed before us. We were asked with other parties to clear the election precondition. We were told that would provide a route, clear and direct, into all-party talks. We have answered that. We came here positively and constructively. We will return.

Barred from the talks despite a renewed mandate — Sinn Féin
at Castle Buildings, Stormont, 1996

Garvaghy siege provokes national outrage

The besieging of the small nationalist community of the Garvaghy Road in Portadown in 1995, '96 and '97 when Orange parades were forced through against their wishes and with the aid of hundreds of RUC and British Army caused outrage in Ireland and internationally.

Caoimhghín Ó Caoláin celebrates his election as TD for Cavan/ Monaghan with Gerry Adams, Martin McGuinness and General Secretary Lucilita Bhreatnach, June 1997.

Two MPs and one TD

The summer of 1997 saw major electoral breakthroughs for Sinn Féin with the re-election of Gerry Adams in West Belfast, the election of Martin McGuinness in Mid-Ulster and Caoimhghín Ó Caoláin topping the poll in Cavan/Monaghan to become Sinn Féin's first participating TD in Leinster House. When the Dáil met on 26 June 1997, Ó Caoláin set out his party's priorities. Solely on the basis of the need to restore the peace process, and considering the negative record of Fine Gael under John Bruton, Sinn Féin voted for Bertie Ahern as Taoiseach. Following the 2002 General Election, with the peace process restored, the party's TDs abstained.

First Dáil speech of Caoimhghín Ó Caoláin

Is páirtí poblachtach é Sinn Féin agus i bhfocail Fhorógra na Poblachta 1916 "dearbhaimid gur ceart ceannasach do-chloíte ceart mhuintir na hÉireann chun tír na hÉireann, agus fós chun dála na hÉireann a stiúradh gan chosc gan toirmeasc".

Níl an cheannasacht iomlán fós ag muintir na hÉireann agus is é bunchuspóir mo pháirtí an Phoblacht uile-Éireannach a chur ar bun.

Tagaim anseo mar ionadaí ó cheantar atá imeallach le fada an lá mar gheall ar chríchdheighilt ar dtíre agus mar gheall ar neamhaird ag rialtais i ndiaidh rialtais sa stát seo. Mar Theachta beidh sé mar bhunaidhm agam deireadh a chur leis an neamhaird sin agus mo cheantar a chur ar ais i lár pholaitíocht na tíre seo.

I am honoured to stand here today, a Cheann Comhairle and fellow Deputies, as a Deputy for the people of Cavan and Monaghan and as a representative of Sinn Féin, the party of which I am proud to be a member. I represent an all-Ireland party that enjoys a significant mandate in both parts of our divided island and I welcome the presence here today of my colleagues, Gerry Adams, MP for West Belfast, and Martin McGuinness, MP for Mid-Ulster. I look forward to the day when I will join them and all the others elected by the Irish people as a whole in a national parliament for the 32 Counties...

In the general election Sinn Féin stood as a party for change. Our vision is of a new Ireland, of people united in shared prosperity. We note the failure of successive administrations in this State to fulfil the aim of the Democratic Programme of the first Dáil Éireann which declared the right of every citizen to an adequate share of the produce of the nation's labour...

Promoting the interests of my constituents in Cavan and Monaghan and advancing the case for a fairer social and economic order based on equality will be my priorities during the course of the term before us. The partition of our country and Britain's occupation of the six north-eastern counties is the single greatest problem facing us as a people. The most important task for us all is to rebuild the peace process. This must include the full recognition of Sinn Féin's electoral mandate by both governments...

One TD and two MPs at Leinster House, 26 June, 1997

Multi-party talks

Over three years after the first IRA cessation, multi-party talks finally commenced. The IRA cessation had been restored in July 1997 but talks were only seriously under way in early 1998. This is from a key party document submitted to the talks on 24 March:

Sinn Féin leadership before their first meeting with the British Government at 10 Downing Street, 13 October 1997.
from left: Martin Ferris, Michelle Gildernew, Martin McGuinness, Gerry Adams, Lucilita Bhreatnach, Siobhan O'Hanlon

We want to end the Union. An Irish Republic represents a model of society on which the people of the island can build a new future for ourselves. There are other models. Which of these is to eventually replace the current set-up is a matter for the people of the island to decide, free from any outside interference or impediments. This is the democratic position. It is one supported by Sinn Féin.

Therefore the broad democratic view of the type of political agreement that will come out of the current talks process is that it must be based in an explicit all-Ireland context. So that even while there is disagreement on the shape of a new Ireland there should be agreement on the peace objective of making the island a better place for all the people who live here. There must be a commitment to the shared objective of removing the causes of conflict. That is one of the stated objectives of this process. It will be a litmus test of any agreement.

South African comrade shares negotiating experience

Thenjiwe Mtintso, the Deputy Secretary General of the ANC, shared the experience of the negotiation process in South Africa with delegates at the 1998 Ard Fheis. Thenjiwe said she experienced a sense of deja vu – the arguments used by the delegates to the Ard Fheis were exactly the same as those used within the ANC in debates over strategy in the early 1990s:

Deputy Secretary General of the ANC, Thenjiwe Mtintso, with Gerry Adams at the 1998 Ard Fheis

It did not matter a bit the type of negotiators we had. Whether they were the best we had, it did not matter; the amount of commitment that the negotiators had, it did not matter; the amount of skill they had did not matter. What mattered was that there was clear consultation and participation of every cadre of the African National Congress in the process. What mattered was the fact that we were able during that period to increase our base beyond that of the African National Congress and to begin to undermine the opposition. We won to our side of the ANC many of the South Africans who were not members of the ANC, who were not members of the alliance, but were people who were committed to transformation and to change in our country.

What was quite critical for us in South Africa was mass mobilisation and mass activism of our people at all levels of our society and in all fronts. In all of that what was key was that negotiations were about one terrain of struggle and that all other terrains of struggle were intact and were getting stronger and stronger. Therefore even as our negotiators were going forward to sit hour after hour with the racist regime they knew that they had not only the support of the ANC and the alliance but the support of the country, the support of the democratic forces in our country...

We in South Africa saw, and still see, because sometimes people talk about the miracle in South Africa, that we had a miracle and the problem with that is that they reduce our struggle to the supernatural. That there was a miracle that happened and suddenly we were free. There was no miracle that happened in South Africa. There was blood and tears of South Africans. There were hours and hours of struggling on all fronts and we accepted negotiations. There were lots of limitations and we are still suffering from some elements of the negotiations, but we saw that as a stage, we saw that as a moment, we saw that as a space which we needed to occupy so that we could surge forward...

The Good Friday Agreement

The multi-party talks concluded with the Good Friday Agreement. Sinn Féin convened its 1998 Ard Fheis in April to hear a report from its negotiators and an analysis of the Agreement. It reconvened in May to formally decide on its attitude to the Agreement. It voted to allow Sinn Féin members to take seats in the new Assembly. In his presidential address, Gerry Adams contextualised the decisions:

Today we decided collectively how we will approach the Good Friday paper. On the one hand it upholds the unionist veto over the constitutional status of the north, and, on the other hand it reduces the British territorial claim to that one hinge while it compels unionists to accept key and fundamental changes involving all-Ireland dimensions to everyday life.

Our negotiating team went into the talks to get the Government of Ireland Act repealed. We succeeded in that. We also secured the inclusion of a clause in the new British constitutional legislation which states that the new act "shall have effect notwithstanding any previous enactment". This includes the Act of Union and the Northern Ireland Constitution Act 1973. There is now no indefinite commitment, no raft of Parliamentary Acts to back up an absolute claim. This is a long way from being as British as Finchley. But British rule has not ended. Neither has partition. That is why our struggle continues.

Because the Act we want to see is the Act which ends the union. We haven't got that yet. But we will. That is the reality.

Today's decision that successful Sinn Féin candidates should participate in the assembly in the north is a historic one. It must be underpinned by a strategy wedded to mobilisations, campaigning, street activism and the international dimension. Caoimhghín Ó Caoláin has set a high standard for all our representatives and we need more constituencies like his throughout the 26 Counties represented by Sinn Féin deputies. The work in the north will assist this but our party is the only national one in Ireland and we have to build our political strength everywhere on this island if we are to secure the national advances we require.

So the struggle has to be where the activist is and it has to be social and economic, as well as political. It has to be about ending poverty, about building an economic democracy, about treating all the children of the nation equally, as well as about ending British rule.

Republican prisoner Hugh Doherty is greeted at the 1998 Ard Fheis, having spent over 20 years in English prisons

Saoirse campaign to free the prisoners

A key element in the peace process for Republicans was the demand for the early release of political prisoners. The campaign became national and international under the banner of Saoirse. Early releases were written into the Good Friday Agreement and a programme of releases was undertaken. But it was a slow process. By the end of 2000, most of the prisoners had been released, although some, such as those in Castlerea, were still being held. In December 1998, a group of prisoners were still being held in Portlaoise Prison, having served over 20 years in English jails before transfer. Eoghan MacCormaic, himself a former prisoner, wrote about them:

As Joe O'Connell, Harry Duggan, Eddie Butler and Hugh Doherty were being held in Paddington Police Station in December 1975, British Home Secretary Roy Jenkins was predicting that some IRA prisoners would be held in jail forever. It must seem now that he was right.

This Saturday, 12 December, marks the beginning of the 24th year of imprisonment for the Balcombe Street Four. A lifetime has gone by, states have fallen, wars fought, technology revolutionised, geography and history books rewritten. After 22 years they were finally transferred and are now in Portlaoise at the behest of the British Government. It's long, long past the time when they should be free.

Electoral gains made but Agreement stalled

Martin Ferris

The Ulster Unionist Party led by David Trimble did not meet face to face with Sinn Féin until February 1999, well after the Good Friday Agreement. They stalled implementation of the Agreement for that entire year. In June, Sinn Féin made significant advances in local elections in the 26 Counties and EU elections throughout Ireland. Martin Ferris, newly elected to Kerry County Council, addressed the Bodenstown commemoration:

It is a fact that there are those within both unionism and the British establishment who are opposed to progress and to the peace process. This opposition is being strengthened and encouraged by the failure to deliver real change and implement the Agreement. The political vacuum, which has existed since the Agreement was made, has created a dangerous and unpredictable situation. It has been filled by the rejectionists, by those within the establishment, the bureaucrats and securocrats, who seek at every opportunity to dilute or delay every proposal for change.

We can see the establishment fighting back in the decision to back anonymity for the Paras who killed innocent civil rights marchers on Bloody Sunday. We can see it in the release of Lee Clegg. We can see it in the failure of the British Government to produce its proposals on demilitarisation. And we can see it in the actions of the British Army in South Armagh and Tyrone and in the behaviour of the RUC.

This vacuum has also been filled by a loyalist campaign of violence and intimidation against nationalists. 10 people have died. Men, women and children. Nationalist communities in East Antrim, South Antrim, Portadown, North Belfast and elsewhere are subject to threats and violence. Scores of families have been bombed and frightened from their homes. School children have been terrorised...

You have a right to be proud of our achievements in the European and local elections. Our vote has risen all over the country and we are now truly an all-Ireland party, growing in strength and confidence. I want to salute each and every one of our election candidates and workers. I salute all of you who gave of your time and efforts to make these tremendous results possible. Those results show that republicanism is alive and well and is relevant to the Ireland of today and, more importantly, the Ireland of tomorrow.

Executive established with two Sinn Féin ministers

The Executive and all-Ireland bodies provided for in the Good Friday Agreement were only finally established on 29 November 1999. Sinn Féin's Ministers were Martin McGuinness (Education) and Bairbre de Brún (Health, Social Services and Public Safety). Gerry Adams addressed the Assembly:

We stand on the threshold of great change... Sinn Féin is proud to stand in the tradition of the Presbyterians of the 1790s who fought for Liberty, Equality and Fraternity. Our goal remains the establishment of a united, free and independent Ireland. We believe the Good Friday Agreement is the transitional structure that will allow us to achieve that legitimate objective. Others in this Assembly will hold a different view. That's fair enough. But what we now have is a means by which we can all pursue our political goals in partnership, as equals, in mutual respect and toleration.

This compromise does not require the compromise of principles or the diminution of vision. What it does require is a focus and a harnessing of energy to bring about visible and fundamental change in people's daily lives.

The Six-County Executive at its inaugural meeting, 1999.

(inset): Minister for Health, Bairbre de Brún and Minster for Education, Martin McGuinness

EUROPEAN ELE
ND **AL ELE**
E CO
AY 12

Newly elected Sinn Féin Councillors Seán
Crowe, Larry O'Toole and Christy Burke
celebrate at the election count centre,
RDS, Dublin, 1999.

New millennium, same old unionism

The beginning of the new millennium in 2000 saw the stepping up of the Unionist campaign of stalling the Good Friday Agreement. They had the assistance of British Secretary of State Peter Mandelson who suspended the Good Friday Agreement institutions in February. They were restored in June but were dogged by Unionist intransigence. The impasse continued into 2001 and, despite IRA initiatives on arms, they were suspended again in August. In the meantime Sinn Féin had historic election successes in June 2001. Joining their three sitting MPs was Michelle Gildernew in Fermanagh/South Tyrone, where Bobby Sands was elected 20 years earlier. The 20th anniversary year of the Hunger Strike was marked at events all around Ireland and worldwide. At a ceremony in Dublin in May, the speaker was one of Bobby's prison comrades, Séanna Bhreatnach.

Séanna Bhreatnach speaking in Glasnevin Cemetery in May 2001

I was 20 in 1976. We were kids. We hadn't the least idea what to do. But we decided we would not wear the prison uniform and we wouldn't do prison work.

It goes back to the time of O'Donovan Rossa, chained for years in Dartmoor Prison with his hands tied behind his back, forced to eat as a dog. We wouldn't allow our struggle to be criminalised. It is so important that young people today know of these times, that they get a sense of the brutality, of the suffering. It is so important that the Hunger Strike experience is not forgotten.

We were only youngsters. We were often head to head with the IRA, who saw what was going on as a distraction and were terrified lest it should lead to a hunger strike.

The hunger strike was as much about those who weren't on hunger strike, the women in Armagh, the thousands who walked the streets day after day....

Newly-elected Fermanagh/ South Tyrone MP, Michelle Gildernew, at Hunger Strike commemoration, Dublin 2001

Holy Cross

2001 saw the face of loyalist bigotry exposed as loyalist mobs taunted and attacked primary school children on their way to Holy Cross School in North Belfast.

Sinn Féin's five TDs on their way into Leinster House, May 2002: Martin Ferris TD Aengus Ó Snodaigh TD, Gerry Adams MP, Pat Doherty MP, Caoimhghín Ó Caoláin TD, Arthur Morgan TD and Seán Crowe TD

Inset: Sinn Féin's four MPs

All-Ireland breakthrough for Sinn Féin

In 2001, Sinn Féin had emerged as the leading nationalist party in the North, overtaking the SDLP. On the same day, the party won four Westminster seats, 108 councillors in the Six Counties and played a key role in securing a 'No' vote in the referendum on the Nice Treaty in the 26 Counties. Then in May 2002 the party won five Dáil seats and began to change the political landscape on an All-Ireland basis. Martin Ferris topped the poll in Kerry North and spoke at the count:

Thirty-two years ago, I became involved in a struggle for equality, justice and peace and for many of those dark years there was no option but pain and suffering for all our people. And I do not want in any way to say that we suffered more than anybody else. People suffered. The enemy suffered, we suffered. And many of those years I spent in prison and many comrades of mine at that time are now dead and at this moment I remember them. I remember them for their comradeship and their commitment to justice.

Sinn Féin Vice-President Pat Doherty and
General Secretary Lucilita Bhreatnach meet
with Palestinian leader Yasser Arafat,
Dublin 2001

Peace process crisis deepens

In one of the most provocative acts during the entire peace process, the RUC/PSNI raided Sinn Féin's offices in Stormont in October 2002. The institutions were suspended again amidst false allegations that Sinn Féin was carrying out espionage within the Assembly and Executive. The following May, the crisis was compounded when the British Government unilaterally cancelled Assembly elections, despite the publicly stated opposition to this move by the Irish Government. In the autumn, Republicans acted again to secure progress. The IRA put a substantial quantity of arms beyond use, verified by the Independent International Commission on Decommissioning. But none of this was enough for David Trimble who refused to fulfil his part of the agreement.

When the Assembly elections were finally held, in November 2003, Sinn Féin's vote increased substantially — up 6% from the 98 Assembly poll.

In his 2004 Ard Fheis presidential speech, Gerry Adams addressed Unionists:

Unionists fear that if given the chance republicans and nationalists would treat them as second-class citizens. We would not, and we will not. The days of second-class citizens are over.

When we demand equality, we demand equality for everyone.

Presidential address at the
2004 Ard Fheis

So, these fears must be dealt with. We have that duty, as do the leaders of unionism. For this reason, Irish republicans are ready to do business with the various unionist camps. The DUP and the UUP, the two largest unionist parties, are involved in a cynical, frustrating exercise in macho posturing.

Ian Paisley and David Trimble are fighting for control of unionism, both trying to prove how tough they are. And while they play their power games, the peace process stalls, and withers.

Sooner or later, we and the unionists must begin a real dialogue, an anti-sectarian dialogue, designed to move us all beyond the impasse of the present into a living, hopeful future in which they, as well as we, tell the British Government to butt-out; that no longer will London, which is not trusted or respected by any constituency in Ireland, set the terms for us.

The DUP is now the senior unionist party. The logic of its position is that it should be in government with Sinn Féin. Republicans are not naïve about the DUP. We know that they want to minimise the process of change.

But the DUP also knows that if it wants a return to sustainable devolved administration that it will be with Sinn Féin in government and it will be with the all-Ireland model contained in the Good Friday Agreement.

So our party is prepared to explore the DUP position, not because we have any illusions about Mr. Paisley's position, but because we have confidence in our own position and because one of our objectives is for a strategic alliance with unionism for the benefit of all our people. We recognise and respect the mandate of the DUP; they must recognise and respect our mandate.

Joe Cahill
1920 - 2004

The dream of freedom — Joe Cahill, 1920-2004

Sinn Féin Honorary Vice-President Joe Cahill died in 2004. His passing marked the end of an era as he had been a central figure in the republican struggle for decades. In 2003, he spoke at a special function organised to honour his life's work and his family:

We all have dreams and we all have desires. A few weeks ago I was being released from the Royal Victoria Hospital. As I was waiting to go down in the lift to the ground floor I happened to look out through the window and I saw the best sight ever of the Cave Hill.

I remember looking at the Cave Hill and I remember thinking that is where it all started. I thought of Tone and his comrades and what they said and what they planned to do. What struck me most was that they wanted to change the name of Protestant, Catholic and Dissenter to Irish people. That started me thinking and then I thought of the people who came after them. Emmet and what he tried to do and the message that he left us. My mind wandered on through the years to the Fenians and one man stuck out in my mind, not a Fenian, but a man called Francis Meagher who brought the flag that we all love, our Tricolour. He said, 'I have brought this flag from the barricades of France and I am presenting it to the Irish nation. Green represents the Catholic, the Orange the Protestant and the white the truce between them.' I hope that one day the hand of Protestant and Catholic will be united and respect that flag.

Then I thought of the Fenians and I thought of the likes of old Tom Clarke and what he had gone through in prison. I remembered that he was the first signatory to the 1916 Proclamation, which says it all as far as we are concerned. Then I thought of the 30s, 40s and what we went through at that time. The struggle we put up then and what we were up against. Right through into the 70s.

People have often asked me 'What keeps you going?'. I think of Bobby Sands and Bobby said 'It is that thing inside me that tells me I'm right.' That's what drives me on. I know we are right. I think also what Bobby said about revenge. There is no revenge on his part. He said that the true revenge would be the laughter of our children.

I think of Tom Williams and the last days that I spent with him in the condemned cell. I think of that letter that he wrote out to his comrades, to the then Chief of Staff, Hugh McAteer. He said the road to freedom would be hard and that many a hurdle on that road would be very difficult. It has been a hard struggle but he said, 'Carry on my comrades until that certain day.'

And that day that he talked about was the dawn of freedom.

Just one other remark I would like to make about Tom. It was his desire, as we all talked together when we were under the sentence of death, that one day our bodies would be taken out of Crumlin Road and laid to rest in Milltown. The reason I mention this at all is this is what determination does. This is what consistency and work does. I personally thought that I would never see Tom's remains coming out until we got rid of the British but people worked hard at that. People worked very, very hard and we got Tom's remains out. So with hard work it shows what you can do.

I don't want to keep you much longer but I too have a dream. In 2005 we will celebrate the 100th anniversary of Sinn Féin. I am not saying we are going to get our freedom by then but certainly we can pave the way by then. We can work hard. And hard work brings results...

I am asking for that continued support not for me but for Sinn Féin, for the Republican Movement which is going to bring about the dreams of Ireland, the dreams of the United Irishmen, the dreams of Emmet, of the Fenians, of the men of '16. The dreams of those who have died through the '30s, the '40s and right into the present day, and I am asking you to continue your support. Whatever little you have done in the past do that wee bit more and we will have our freedom.

Martin McGuinness and Gerry Adams at the funeral of Joe Cahill

2 MEPs, 252 Councillors, 24 MLAs, 5 TDs and 5 MPs

In the May 2005 Westminster election, Sinn Féin gained a seat in Newry/Armagh. The new MP, Conor Murphy, addressed the implications of the election results for the peace process:

What it should mean, particularly in the absence of a proper elected institution in the North, is the beginning of a campaign to get representation in the Dáil. That has always been the Sinn Féin position — for all nationalists to lobby the Dublin Government to give Northern citizens full and proper representation in Southern institutions.

The SDLP obviously plan to take their oaths in Westminster and I think that's very regrettable. If the collective strength we now have could be harmonised, it could be used to advance the cause of Irish citizens North and South of the border.

The fact that there's always been a lack of enthusiasm from the SDLP and the Irish Government in this area has always been a deep regret for republicans.

Nationalism should also now be focusing on ensuring that the areas of the Good Friday Agreement, which have been neglected so far by the Irish and British governments, are implemented, including demilitarisation, policing, human rights and equality.

And then, collectively, we should be getting the DUP involved so we can get the institutions up and running again.

Whether any of this will happen, or whether the work will be left to Sinn Féin again, remains to be seen.

Newly elected Sinn Féin MP, Conor Murphy (left), with fellow candidates Alex Maskey MLA, Caitríona Ruane MLA and Mitchel McLaughlin MLA, June 2005

Right to left: Sinn Féin MEPs Mary Lou McDonald and Bairbre de Brún, Munster EU Candidate Cllr. David Cullinane and Gerry Adams at Bodenstown 2004

The five Sinn Féin MPs elected in May 2005 (left to righ Pat Doherty, Martin McGuinness, Gerry Adams, Michel Gildernew and Conor Murphy with MEP Mary Lou McDonald in London for talks with the British Prime Minster, Tony Blair